Slavery, Resistance, Freedom

Gettysburg Civil War Institute Books
Published by Oxford University Press
Edited by Gabor Boritt

Why the Confederacy Lost

Lincoln, the War President

Lincoln's Generals

War Comes Again

Why the Civil War Came

The Gettysbury Nobody Knows

Jefferson Davis's Generals

The Lincoln Enigma

Other books by Gabor Boritt

The Gettysburg Gospel: The Lincoln Speech that Nobody Knows

Lincoln and the Economics of the American Dream

The Lincoln Image
(with Harold Holzer and Mark E. Neely, Jr.)

The Confederate Image
(with Mark E. Neely, Jr., and Harold Holzer)

The Historian's Lincoln
(with Norman O. Forness)

The Historian's Lincoln, Rebuttals:
What the University Press Would Not Print

Of the People, By the People, For the People
and Other Quotations from Abraham Lincoln
(with Jakob B. Boritt, Deborah R. Huson, and Peter C. Vermilyea)

Slavery, Resistance, Freedom

EDITED BY

GABOR BORITT
and SCOTT HANCOCK

ESSAYS BY

Ira Berlin

John Hope Franklin and Loren Schweninger

Scott Hancock

Edward L. Ayers, William G. Thomas III,
and Anne Sarah Rubin

Noah Andre Trudeau

Eric Foner

OXFORD
UNIVERSITY PRESS

2007

OXFORD
UNIVERSITY PRESS

Oxford University Press, Inc., publishes works that
further Oxford University's objective of excellence
in research, scholarship, and education.

Oxford   New York
Auckland   Cape Town   Dar es Salaam   Hong Kong   Karachi
Kuala Lumpur   Madrid   Melbourne   Mexico City   Nairobi
New Delhi   Shanghai   Taipei   Toronto

With offices in
Argentina   Austria   Brazil   Chile   Czech Republic   France   Greece
Guatemala   Hungary   Italy   Japan   Poland   Portugal   Singapore
South Korea   Switzerland   Thailand   Turkey   Ukraine   Vietnam

Copyright © 2007 by Gabor Boritt

Published by Oxford University Press, Inc.
198 Madison Avenue, New York, NY 10016
www.oup.com

Oxford is a registered trademark of Oxford University Press

Library of Congress Cataloging-in-Publication Data
Slavery, resistance, freedom / edited by Gabor S. Boritt ; Scott Hancock,
assistant editor ; essays by Ira Berlin . . . [et al.].
p. cm.
Includes bibliographical references.
ISBN 978-0-19-510222-2
1. Slavery—United States—History.   2. Slavery—United States—Historiography.
3. Memory—Social aspects—United States—History.   4. Government, Resistance to—
United States—History.   5. Fugitive slaves—United States—History.   6. Slave
insurrections—United States—History.   7. African Americans—Social conditions—To
1964.   8. United States—History—Civil War, 1861–1865—Participation, African
American.   9. African American leadership—History—19th century.   10. Reconstruction
(U.S. history, 1865–1877)   I. Boritt, G. S., 1940-   II. Hancock, Scott.   III. Berlin,
Ira, 1941–
E441.S644 2007
326.0973—dc22   2006038009

Map on page 104 © 2004 Noah Andre Trudeau

9 8 7 6 5 4 3 2

Printed in the United States of America
on acid-free paper

To Tom Kemp and Ed Johnson

By late June it is usually warm,
Even hot in Gettysburg.
In the night at our farm,
The fireflies glow in the dark,
Fleeting specks illuminating the woods and
Turning Marsh Creek into a pageant.
In the daytime along the side of the road,
Orange tiger lilies proclaim their eternal message.
My heart overflows;
It is time to see old friends again,
Time to make new ones.
It is time for the Gettysburg Civil War Institute.

GABOR BORITT

Contents

Acknowledgments

A<small>LL</small> <small>KNEW</small>," Lincoln said in the spring of 1865, that slavery "was, somehow, the cause of the war."[1] That war, the only one in the history of the United States in which all participants were Americans, cost more than six hundred twenty thousand dead, and a million and a half in total casualties. In a like war today, in a nation with a population of three hundred million people, those numbers would grow, proportionally, to five and a half million dead, and more than thirteen million in total casualties.

Those soul-shattering figures point to one of the costs of American slavery. Of course Lincoln was wrong in saying that "all" knew. Neither then nor now do all know, though in our time most professional historians, at least, have come to accept the centrality of slavery to the Civil War. Indeed scholars have gone further, taking the words of Lincoln's second inaugural address to their logical conclusion by picturing the institution of slavery as crucial to all of U.S. history. However uncomfortable that thought still is in this twenty-first century, we can take comfort in knowing that Americans are trying to face up to the issues spawned by this, the most dominant flaw of a truly remarkable history.

At Gettysburg, we celebrated the twentieth anniversary of the founding of the Civil War Institute at Gettysburg College by devoting a weeklong session to African American history. Some of the finest experts came together to speak and debate the subject in its Civil War context. Also, on each November 19 we remember the Gettysburg Address as an academic institution should, by inviting a leading scholar of the Civil War era to give a lecture. The visiting historians often focus on slavery. This book brings together many of these lectures to form a volume that sheds important light on slavery, resistance, and freedom. The fact that the book's progression leads toward freedom testifies to American history. To quote the introduction written by my colleague Scott Hancock, "Though perspectives on how much freedom has been realized differ, and though desire for freedom is far from being uniquely American, striving for freedom has shaped much of what it means to be an American. The ideal has made a difference."

And now to thank people who helped bring this book to life. The Civil War Institute (CWI) continues to be a happy, very hard-working place, and my first thanks go to the fine staff led by Tina Grim, aided by Diane Brennan, Pam Dalrymple, and my personal assistant Susan Oyler—all outstanding people in their own ways. Susan deserves special thanks for helping to see the manuscript through publication.

The CWI sessions attract wonderful, interesting people from as far away as Alaska and Australia, ranging in age from the teens to nearly ninety. What a pleasure it is to learn with them and to share their company. We also present scholarships to both rising high-school seniors and teachers. Their work is supervised and enriched by Pete Vermilyea and Bill Hanna. Better helpers and friends one need not hope for.

Student assistants, all Gettysburg College undergraduates, play an important part in the life of the CWI, make it great fun, and it is a pleasure to thank them all. At the session devoted to African American history, the assistants included Gerrit L. Blauvelt, Cora R. Chandler, Eric Esser, Ian P. Harkness, Nancy Moll, Theresa L. Obyle, Timothy S. Parry II, Jason E. Patton, Jared E. Peatman, Kathryn S. Porch, and Heidi Schuster.

Many of these students also assisted my work over the years, some paid and some as volunteers, providing so much help that I can barely conceive of my life without their hard work and blithe spirits. Their troop also includes Andrew Douglas, Emily Hummel, and Craig Schneider. Thank you.

Next I thank my family. Liz, my wife, only grows as my source of strength. Our boys, though now living far away, remain an integral part of our family. Norse and his wife, Mimi, always take time from their hectic lives in the theater in the Big Apple for happy times together. Jake, a fine young documentary filmmaker also based in New York, roams the globe, but ever remains a friend and a liberating intellectual companion. Dan, the youngest, at the Bird Department of the National Zoo in Washington, adds spice to our lives—even when he is on a Smithsonian expedition to Antartica, as he is now. Together they help make life and so the creating of books meaningful.

One of the great pleasures of being a professor is to see talented younger colleagues coming along. I'm delighted to have a companion in bringing this book before the reading public. Scott Hancock joined the Gettysburg History Department in 2001, quickly making himself into a fine, helpful colleague. As a teacher of African American history, he brings special sensibilities to our work. His introduction to the book follows.

Autumn 2006   Gabor Boritt
Farm by the Ford
Gettysburg

Introduction

Whenever I teach survey classes in American History, I inevitably ask students what it means to them to be an American. The answers are deceivingly brief. Though limited to a sentence or two, they betray a deep consciousness of American history. Unsurprisingly, students of diverse backgrounds—young and old, white and black, male and female, American citizens and other nationalities—typically describe American identity as being centered on freedom: of speech, of worship, of pursuit of opportunity. It is a response with an illusory, ubiquitous, yet profound simplicity. Though perspectives on how much freedom has been realized differ and though desire for freedom is far from being uniquely American, striving for freedom has shaped much of what it means to be an American. The ideal has made a difference.

These chapters, to adapt a title by a recent work of Edward Ayers and William Thomas, tell stories of the difference that freedom—and slavery—have made.[1] They tell the stories of that difference as the nation struggled to resolve how it could live with these polar opposites, and how Americans have dealt with the memory of that struggle.

The chapters especially focus on the difference that slavery and freedom made to African Americans, and how African Americans resisted slavery and responded when it crumbled. It is not simply a story of triumph or defeat. In 1867, William Wells Brown, an African American writer, speaker, and fiery leader who had escaped slavery himself, published *The Negro in the American Rebellion.* At the conclusion of his chapter on Nat Turner's ill-fated slave rebellion in 1831, he told the story of Jim, a slave to one of the leaders who pursued Nat Turner and his band of rebels. This slave owner owed his life to Jim, for Jim had given him sufficient warning that Turner's band was coming. The slave owner took Jim with him to help hunt down Nat Turner's men. But Jim drew a line. "I cannot help you hunt down these men," he said, for "they, like myself, want to be free." Jim had reached his breaking point. Handing his gun to his master, he told him to "please give me my freedom, or shoot me on the spot." Jim was probably trying to read his master, but also likely meant exactly what he said. For him, life without freedom was not a life worth living. Thousands of other black men and women reached that point and attempted to escape North. Far more did not run away but, like Jim, contested slavery on some level. Some lost their lives. Jim did not survive his personal contest. Despite having saved his master's life, his own life was not saved.[2] A few slaves did gain freedom; most continued to struggle to moderate their circumstances in order to make life tolerable. Black women and men's struggles against slavery ultimately contributed to their emancipation—though the struggle did not end there.

The impact of African Americans' struggle with slavery and their efforts to make a place for themselves in the post–Civil War United States shaped the nation then, and persists in doing so today. Ira Berlin's chapter begins at the dawn of the twenty-first century. He demonstrates that slavery continues to play a vital role in the public discourse of both popular culture and politics in the United States. Over one hundred thirty-five years after slavery's legal demise, Americans' reactions to it range from curious to willfully ignorant, passionate to purposefully disinterested, bitter to hopeful. Berlin pursues the question of why slavery has remained rooted not only in the consciousness of people prone to gloss over unsightly blemishes in our nation's past, but also why it continues to provoke strong responses. He suggests that slavery has become a surrogate for Americans' often frustrating public and private discourses on race. But historians' study of slavery has only begun to explore adequately the totality of hundreds of years of experience. If slavery has become a way of talking about race, then the history of slavery is crucial. In other words, how we remember slavery heavily influences how we discuss race. But, as Berlin points out, memory and history, while inextricably linked, are far from identical. In this chapter, Berlin provides insight for understanding the relationship between memory and history, and how scholars might more accurately inform the memory of slavery's history.

Recently, there has been a growing public interest in one area that shapes our understanding of slavery and African Americans' responses: the stories of runaway slaves. John Hope Franklin and Loren Schweninger demonstrate the complexity of the deceptively simple term "runaway slave." Though historians have long known that black men, women, and children did not always escape in order to get North of the Mason-Dixon line, there have been few studies that condense their multiple motives and actions into one accessible chapter. By fitting together pieces of stories, the authors recreate the landscape that absconding slaves had to live on and off of. Franklin and Schweninger also illuminate the topography of tension that these men and women built up over decades. They suggest that while runaway slaves did prompt fears of insurrection, they more commonly heightened white anxiety regarding the difficulty of ensuring the institution's stability and persistence. The role of runaway slaves as a part of the mounting stresses that eventually exploded in 1861 has not been fully appreciated. Here Franklin and Schweninger point to what their larger work, the Lincoln Prize–winning *Runaway Slaves: Rebels on the Plantation*, makes plain: that slaves' persistence in pushing for temporary or permanent forms of freedom strained slave owners, the South, and the nation.[3]

Free black Northerners also contributed to the strains pushing the country toward disunion. Black leaders in the North, many of whom had Southern roots and would influence postwar leadership in the South, began pushing the country to fulfill the ideals of the Declaration of Independence and the Bill of Rights early on. As a part of that protest, black leaders helped define what it meant to be African American. It meant not only incorporating the ideal of freedom, but also an obligation to fight for individual and corporate freedom. My chapter points out that black leaders' construction of a black identity rested in large part on creating a cohesive memory of African Americans' past. I explore how memory is shaped, and how black leaders wrestled with weaving themselves into the same American fabric that shrouded many of their black brothers and sisters in slavery while maintaining the commitment they had made to shred it.[4]

In "Black on the Border," Edward Ayers, Anne Rubin, and William Thomas examine two counties' experiences in the war that finally ended slavery. They describe the wartime experiences of the residents and inform us not just about the past but also how future research might be expanded. The authors created the outstanding Valley of the Shadow Web site, which contains a bounty of primary source material that reveals the past in Franklin and Augusta counties. Their essay relies almost entirely on this Web site for sources. This chapter is not as heavily imbued with secondary sources as some of the other chapters in this volume, and therefore illuminates intriguing future possibilities for historiography as top-notch Web sites and other well-designed technology make primary sources far more accessible to seasoned scholars, graduate students, and lay people.[5]

Ayers, Thomas, and Rubin also remind us that the boundary between North and South was simultaneously fluid and fixed and that African Americans played a central role in this paradox. The two counties shared a great deal culturally and geographically, and Confederate and Union ventures across the border were not restricted to Lee's advance prior to the Gettysburg campaign. Yet the legal status of black people could not have been more diametrically opposed. In many respects, African Americans were the fulcrum upon which these two counties teetered and were the difference that divided. On the Northern side, whites supported the cause of black freedom or disparaged it, and black men pushed the issue by enlisting at the first opportunity. On the Southern side of the border, the voices of slaves are not present as the voices of free blacks in Franklin are. But the authors make the black presence clear. Slaves' desire for freedom pushed white Southerners in the county to consider the consequences of enlisting them before war broke out. This chapter puts the black residents of the border area in the center of the military and ideological struggle during the Civil War.

For many African American men, freedom represented the opportunity to risk their lives in the fight for greater freedom. In recent years, black troops that served in the Civil War have received increased attention from popular and academic historians. Bridging the gap between these two groups, Noah Andre Trudeau tracks the uneven fortunes of one group of soldiers that was unique among all black troops. The Third Division of the Ninth Corps operated as a part of "the elite white club known as the Army of the Potomac" and was the only black division incorporated into a major Union army. This integrationist "experiment," as Trudeau labels it, did not last and had a mixed record of military accomplishment. The Third Division played a key role in the Crater fiasco in which almost a third of the black troops were killed or wounded. But the division also eventually demonstrated to both white and black Americans that they knew how to perform effectively as a fighting unit.

Trudeau's chapter provides an essential balance for a book that explores the social, mental, and political worlds of African Americans in this momentous age of transition. The war became the driving force that moved them from slavery to freedom. And the sacrifices made by African Americans, especially as military participants, demands a weighty role in any examination of what freedom meant.

After the war, freedom presented real opportunities for African Americans to gain significant political power. Eric Foner has done more than any other historian to correct lingering Reconstruction-era images of freed black people as incompetent and ignorant public servants. Here he provides a glimpse of an impressive array of biographical portraits compiled in his larger work, *Freedom's Lawmakers*. These portraits help ensure that disturbingly persistent images of freed people are "irrevocably laid to rest." African Americans held hundreds of offices across the South, serving as everything from justices of the peace to United States senators. Many had substantial education; others came from more humble backgrounds. They overwhelmingly demonstrated that they were capable of both governing in and maneuvering through the political realm.[6]

Though a disproportionate number of Reconstruction African American leaders were free before national emancipation, they still represented, for a time, the fruition of a popular American ideology: that people from all walks of life could aspire to high office. They demonstrated that the nation's leaders could fully represent its people by being a government by the people, for the people, and truly of the people. Until now, black leaders of that era have not been sufficiently understood as epitomizing the American ideal, but Foner's introduction to these leaders and their tenure in office begins to correct persistent but antiquated misperceptions.

Together the chapters here point to the rich diversity of African Americans' experiences with and responses to freedom and slavery in the Civil War era. We know that black people, both slave and free, resisted all kinds of exploitation and degradation. How they did so, and what that has meant for them and for the nation, defined the struggle from slavery to freedom.

Recently I dragged myself up the several flights of stairs of an observation tower overlooking the Gettysburg battlefields. My youngest son, barely a teenager, led the way. At the top, as we surveyed green fields laying under the high wispy clouds of a pleasantly blue sky, we read about Pickett's Charge, the Peach Orchard, and the Highwater mark. All are figurative and literal landmarks in American history. I was struck once again by how many young men never walked off those fields and how many lives of families and friends were forever shattered—all because of black men, women, and children. I commented on this to my son, who thought for a second and then said, "Well, that's not true. They weren't fighting just because of black people. They were fighting because the South didn't want to be a part of the country, and the North didn't think the country could survive if they let the South go." I pointed out one simple reality to him—if there were no black people in this country, if Africans had never been forced to these shores, there would have been no Civil War. In fact, there would be no United States as we now know it. The battlefield at Gettysburg epitomizes this reality in many respects. Though physically absent from the battle, African Americans—along with the soldiers, the laborers, the abolitionists, the slaveholders, the political leaders, the mothers, fathers, sons, and daughters—are very much at the heart of the story.

In some African societies, a man who did not know his history was viewed as a man who did not know himself and was therefore not deserving of respect. Knowing one's history meant more than simply reciting names and dates. It meant knowing the stories. It meant knowing what and why things happened, and understanding the significance of those events. One cannot fully know American history, much less the history of the Civil War era, without knowing the stories of African Americans as they, like the rest of the nation, struggled with slavery, resistance, and freedom. These chapters build from that perspective.

Slavery,
Resistance,
Freedom

1

American Slavery in History and Memory

IRA BERLIN

*Tho' de slave question am settled, de race question will be
wid us always, 'till Jesus come de second time. It's in our
politics, in our justice courts, on our highways, on our side
walks, in our manners, in our 'ligion, and in our thoughts,
all de day and every day.*
CORNELIUS HOLMES, WINNSBORO, S.C.

THE RATIFICATION of the Thirteenth Amendment to the
Constitution in December 1865 abolished slavery in the United
States. In the years that followed, Southern planters and their allies
proved extraordinarily resourceful in inventing new forms of labor
extraction and racial oppression, but—try as they might—they
could not reinstate chattel bondage. Yet, almost a century and a
half later, the question of slavery again roils the water of American
life. Indeed, the last years of the twentieth and the first years of the
twenty-first centuries have witnessed an extraordinary popular
engagement with slavery. Slavery has a greater presence in American
life now than at any time since the Civil War ended.

1

The new interest in slavery has been manifested in the success on the big screen of the movies *Glory, Amistad, Shadrach,* and Oprah Winfrey's blockbuster, *Beloved.* They were followed on the small screen by the four-part TV series, *Africans in America,* which traced the history of slavery in Henry Louis Gates's controversial sojourn through Africa, where he confronted the painful matter of African complicity in the trans-Atlantic slave trade.[1] The television docudramas were paralleled by any number of radio broadcasts of which *Remembering Slavery: African Americans Talk about their Personal Experiences in Slavery and Freedom*—a collaboration of scholars (including myself) at the University of Maryland, the Smithsonian Institution, and the Library of Congress—was but one.[2] These broadcasts, in turn, came hard on the heels of John Vlach's "The Back of the Big House" exhibit at the Library of Congress and a presentation of the famous Augustus Saint Gaudens' frieze of the Massachusetts Fifty-fourth at the National Gallery. At present, workers in Washington, D.C., are putting the finishing touches on a monument to Civil War black soldiers styled after the Vietnam memorial—listing the names of all two hundred thousand soldiers and sailors, most of them former slaves.[3] A monument to the *Amistad* captives stands in front of City Hall in New Haven, and the *Amistad* itself has been reconstructed at Mystic Seaport in Connecticut. Recently launched, it began its journey of reconciliation down the East Coast, stopping at major ports of call. For like reasons, United Nations Educational, Scientific, and Cultural Organization's (UNESCO's) slave-trade project is presently installing a string of similar shrines from Africa to the Antilles, some of which will be connected to larger sites of remembrance. In the United States, one such site, the multimillion dollar National Underground Railroad Freedom Center, is under construction in Cincinnati. Others are proposed for Fredericksburg (Virginia), Charleston, and Washington, D.C.—where its supporters hope it will take its place next to the other great commemorations to the American experience on the national mall. When these great museums are completed, they will take their place next to dozens of smaller ones as well as hundreds of freedom trails that trace the movement of fugitives from slavery to freedom.[4]

Historic sites like Belle Grove, Montpelier, Mount Vernon in Virginia; Drayton Hall and the Middleton Place in South Carolina; the Hermitage in Tennessee; Shadow of the Teche in Louisiana; and the Decatur and Octagon houses in Washington once recounted only the story of the great men and women who rambled through their hallways, ate from fine china, and slept in plump feather beds. Now the history of those who were lodged in the basement, ate from wooden bowls, and slept in hammocks or hard pallets has become part of the regimen that is also being told. Such matters are not only the concern of the keepers of these private estates. As is well known at Gettysburg, Congress—in an extraordinary action—has required the National Park Service to address the question of slavery at the appropriate national battlefields. In so doing, the new law returned the nation's sacred grounds to their first purposes, to act as markers of the deep-rooted differences between slavery and freedom. This is far different than the celebration of shared valor. Indeed, transforming the nation's sacred grounds requires more than a new historiography or pedagogy—as became evident in the park service's "Rally on the High Ground." Rather, as Lincoln understood when he first visited Gettysburg, these sacred grounds must become sites of reconciliation and healing.[5]

In the past year, according to the Gilder-Lehrman Institute for the Study of Slavery, Resistance, and Abolition at Yale University (itself evidence of the new interest in slavery), some sixty scholarly books on slavery and related subjects have been published. These are apparently not enough, for the Institute has offered a $50,000 prize for the best book on slavery—in part to encourage further work in the field.[6] To these scholarly works, any number of novels, texts, children's books, chronologies, and genealogies can be added—as well as hundreds of Web sites, dozens of CDs, and at least two operas. Slavery has been on the cover of *Time* and

Newsweek, above the fold in the *Washington Post*, and the lead story on the News of the Week section of the Sunday *New York Times*. And if that were not enough, there was the discovery of what might be termed Sally Hemings's blue dress, and the subsequent and continuing controversy of the paternity of Sally Hemings's children.[7]

The controversy stirred by Sally Hemings's blue dress provides a reminder of how much slavery has become a part of contemporary politics. Bill Clinton recognized this early on and eventually delivered "The Apology" at a former slave factory at Goree on the west coast of Africa. Actually, it is not clear what Clinton said at Goree, since the American media reported the event so poorly. But the political impact of his speech became obvious when a debate—or phantom debate—over The Apology ensued, and conservative congressmen demanded that Clinton retract it.[8] As the haze of dueling editorials over Clinton's remarks faded, the National Advisory Panel on Race Relations, (chaired by the distinguished historian John Hope Franklin), hoved into view.[9] When the panel's report also flagged (literally), the dispute over the Confederate banner in South Carolina erupted and soon spread to neighboring Georgia and Mississippi. In Mississippi, a contentious plebiscite over the state flag roiled the political waters.[10] A like dispute in Virginia over the naming of April as Confederate History Month embarrassed the governor and set loose another long controversy, as did Virginia's state song with its cheerful reference to "darkies" and "ole massa."[11] Perhaps to avoid such a controversy, although maybe to prove the Potomac River still divides the states that stood with the Union and those that joined the Confederacy, Maryland has appointed a Commission for the Study and Commemoration of Slavery. It is the first in the nation, although doubtless not the last as the contemporary politicization of slavery continues to gain momentum.[12]

As the twenty-first century is aborning, the press and the evening news serve up some new controversy over slavery nearly every day. In Washington, D.C., it is the discovery that slaves built the national capitol building.[13] New Yorkers have found that the entire end of Manhattan Island is underlain with the bones of slaves.[14] Students at Yale University uncovered slave owners and slave traders among the university's most prominent founders and benefactors.[15] A suit against the Aetna Insurance Company for insuring slave property a century earlier has not only unleashed a host of similar legal actions but prompted the California legislature to require all insurance companies doing business in the state to reveal if they have insured slave property.[16] Insurance companies are not the only corporate entities at risk. The accusation against Aetna encouraged the *Hartford Courant*, one of the oldest newspapers in the nation, to apologize for advertising slaves for sale.[17] These events resonate daily in the press. Even as I was putting the finishing touches on this essay, the discovery of a new slave narrative appeared on the front page of the Sunday *New York Times*, and the cities of Detroit, Michigan, and Windsor, Ontario, dedicated the first International Underground Railroad Memorial.[18] Lurking behind these public events wait debates over thousands of schools named for Confederate generals and slaveholding politicians (including the most revered leaders in American history), and the vexed and troubled question of reparations.[19]

Although these matters seem to appear and disappear without reason, they reflect no fleeting engagement. Not all that long ago, a story on the front page of the *Washington Post* told about the living history performance that roiled Colonial Williamsburg. The enactment began with a slave auction. The local chapter of the NAACP objected to the reenactment as not only in bad taste, but also insulting and harmful to people of African descent—a painful reminder of what no one wanted to be reminded. The director of the project, Christy Mathews, presently the curator of the African American Museum in Detroit, refused to retreat, insisting that slavery was part of the history of Colonial Williamsburg. The program was not without controversy but the NAACP has since conceded Ms. Mathews's point. The results have been astounding as visitors to Colonial Williamsburg became caught up in the re-enactment and in all of the complicated ways that slavery and its memory touches Americans, both white and black. Some audience members have stepped forward and offered to help slaves escape, others to protect slaves from abusive masters, and some even turned on owners—not merely to debate the issue. Indeed, several visitors had to be physically restrained. Lest it be thought that it is only the visitors who forgot that they had witnessed an enactment, the actors themselves—mostly young black men and women—have been caught up in the drama as well.[20] By playing slaves, they found they were often treated as slaves—not merely by visitors, but by others as well—setting in motion depressing, nightmarish fantasies.

It is rare for Americans to embrace their history, especially at this level of intensity and with this degree of persistence. As a people, the past has not been of great concern to Americans, especially a painful aspect of the past. It is useful to ask why.

Surely part of the reason for the explosion of popular interest in America's slave past has something to do with the recognition of the sheer weight of slavery's importance. Simply put, American history cannot be understood without understanding slavery. Slavery shaped the American economy, its politics, its culture, and its fundamental principles. For most of American history, the mainland colonies and then the United States was a society of slaveholders and slaves.

The American economy was founded upon the production of slave-grown crops: the great staples of tobacco, rice, sugar, and finally cotton that slave owners sold on the international market to bring capital into the colonies and then the young republic. That capital eventually funded the creation of an infrastructure upon which rest three centuries of American economic success.

The great wealth slavery produced allowed slave owners to secure a central role in the establishment of the new federal government in 1787, as they quickly transformed their economic power into political power. Between the founding of the republic and the Civil War, the majority of the presidents—everyone from Washington, Jefferson, Madison, Monroe, Jackson through Tyler, Polk and Taylor—were slaveholders, and generally substantial ones. The same was true for members of the Supreme Court, where a slaveholding majority was ruled over successively by two slaveholding chief justices—John Marshall and Roger Taney—for most of the period between the ratification of the Constitution and the Civil War. A similar pattern can be found in Congress, and it was the struggle for control of Congress between North and South around which antebellum politics revolved.[21]

The power of the slave-owning class, represented by the predominance of slaveholders in the nation's leadership, gave them a large hand in shaping American culture and the values that were associated with American society. It is not an accident that a slaveholder penned the founding statement of American nationality and that freedom became central to the ideology of American nationhood. Men and women who drove slaves understood the meaning of chattel bondage, as most certainly did the men and women who were in fact chattel. And if it is no accident that Thomas Jefferson wrote that "all men are created equal," then it is most certainly no accident that the greatest spokesmen for that ideal from Richard Allen through Frederick Douglass and from W. E. B. Du Bois to Martin Luther King, Jr., were former slaves and the descendants of slaves. The centrality of slavery in the American past is manifest.

It would be comforting to conclude that a recognition of slavery's importance has driven the American people to the history books. But there is more to it than that. There is also a recognition, often backhand and indirect, sometimes subliminal or even subconscious that America's largest, most pervasive social problem—what W. E. B. Du Bois called the great problem of the twentieth century, and that is fast on its way to becoming the great problem of the twenty-first century, that is, racism—is founded in the institution of slavery.[22] There is a general, if inchoate understanding that any attempt to address the question of race in the present must also address slavery in the past. Indeed, Du Bois's racial imperative has become all the more compelling as the United States becomes more racially segregated, more unequal, and as a previous generation's remedies for segregation and inequality are discarded as politically unacceptable. In short, behind the interest in slavery is a crisis of race.[23]

The confluence of the history of slavery and the politics of race suggest that slavery has become a language—a way to talk about race—in a society in which black people and white people hardly talk at all, except perhaps for the banter of sports and the sorry groan of daytime television. Through slavery, Americans, black and white, have found a voice to address some of their deepest hurts, festering anger, and the all-too-depressing reality of how much of American life—access to jobs, housing, schools, medical care, justice, and even a taxi—is still controlled by race. The renaissance in the interest in slavery—in movies, TV docudramas, books, museum exhibits, monuments, and living history reenactments—exemplifies the failure to deal directly with the question of race.

Of course, employing slavery in this manner does not always clarify matters. Take, for example, the dispute over John Vlach's "Behind the Big House" exhibit, an exemplary presentation of slave housing by a premier folklorist drawn from Vlach's fine book of the same title. Its placement in the Library of Congress angered employees of the library—mostly black nonprofessionals—who demanded its removal. They saw in the pictures of the slave quarters a representation of the plantation metaphor they employed to describe their stormy relationship with the Library's administration. The librarian of Congress, a historian by training and trade, acceded to that demand. But, no sooner had the exhibit been dismantled than the librarians at the Martin Luther King, Jr., Library of the District of Columbia—again mostly black—welcomed it and made it a centerpiece of their Black History Month commemoration.[24] A similar double-take is found in the cinematic rendition of Toni Morrison's *Beloved*, which dropped off the edge of the box-office charts only to be proclaimed a critical success, at least in part because of its frank depiction of the extremes to which slavery pushed black people.[25]

If slavery has come from behind the curtains or out of the closet in dozens of historical sites, it has not emerged gracefully. At each of these sites, there have been tense debates over how to present slavery—then charges that interpreters have said too much (Why do you dwell upon it?) or said too little (Why can't you face the truth?). Little wonder that the debate over "The Apology" began with great fanfare and ended in muffled silence, or that the National Park Service has struggled with the congressional mandate, or that the white Jeffersons could not come to terms with the black Jeffersons over access to Monticello's graveyard.[26] The fact that some of the black Jeffersons are whiter to the eye than the white Jeffersons only reveals the knurled complexity of race relations in the United States and suggests that Marx was right. History does repeat itself, first as tragedy, then as farce.

These vexed cases demonstrate how the discussion of slavery is not an easy one. While slavery serves as an entry point for a dialogue on race, it also carries with it deep anger, resentment, indignation, and bitterness for some, and embarrassment, humiliation, and shame for others, along with large drafts of denial—sometimes through evasion or silence. The depths of denial appear to be fathomless, as Americans selectively construct their history: the *Mayflower* is me, the slave ship *Brooks* is not; freedom fighters at Valley Forge are me, those at Southampton are not; freedom is me, slavery is not.

Even as slavery serves as a surrogate for race in these dialogues, it too becomes tangled in the same emotional brier patch. Discussions of slavery are also muted by fears of embarrassment—personal and political—and this is not just a matter of good manners. After more than one-hundred-thirty-plus years since slavery's demise, the weight of slavery's past remains a tender and sensitive subject. It is so sensitive that many Americans cannot even say the word. For some, slavery is disguised by the terms "servants" or "servitude," a recognition of subordination, but an obfuscation of the slave's unique status as property. For others, "slavery" becomes "enslaved people," or more awkward still, "enslaved circumstance," a recognition of the slave's humanity and a pointed denial of the slave's consent to enslavement, but a similar beclouding of the unique meaning of property-in-man. As the struggle over nomenclature reveals, Americans, white and black, feel the need to address the subject of slavery, to understand it, but they do not exactly know how.

A good deal of the difficulty lies in a confusion between slavery's history and slavery's memory—the ways they are connected and the ways they are different. It is those differences that I would like to explore.

Start with the history of slavery in the United States, where scholars have detached slavery from its Civil War nexus and extended its reach across the Atlantic. From this perspective, chattel bondage in the United States has taken on a new look. For most of slavery's history, it was not a Southern institution or a "peculiar institution." Rather, slavery extended across the continent and was embraced, almost without question, by nearly everyone save the slaves themselves. Indeed, for most of its history, those matters that were understood as the touchstones of slavery in the United States—cotton, the Deep South, and the African-Christian church—do not exist. The conventional wisdom—what every school child knows about slavery—is of little help in understanding most of the history of slavery.[27]

Slavery in the United States simply was not what the history books said it was. Rather than being linked exclusively to cotton, the Black Belt, and Afro-Christianity, the slave experience was diverse and volatile, changing over time and through space. Indeed, the rapid mutation of slavery over its three-hundred-year-plus history has required scholars to rethink the institution and the experience of the men and women, masters and slaves who lived it. For myself, I have found it useful to divide that experience into generations: Charter, Plantation, Revolutionary, Migration, and Freedom generations. These diverse experiences successively reshaped the lives of slaves and everyone connected to the institution of slavery, be they slave owners, non-slaveholding whites, or free people of color.

The Charter Generation refers to people of African descent who arrived as slaves in mainland North America prior to the advent of the plantation. Disproportionately, they were people not of the African interior but of the Atlantic coast. Their world focused outward onto the larger Atlantic. They spoke—among other languages—the Creole dialect that had developed among the peoples of the Atlantic in the fifteenth and sixteenth centuries—a language with a Portuguese grammar and syntax, but a vocabulary borrowed from every shore of the Atlantic. They understood something about the trading etiquettes, the religions, and the laws of the Atlantic world. Many of them were employed as interpreters, supercargos, sailors, and compodores—a kind of an all-purpose seaboard handyman—for the great sixteenth- and seventeenth-century trading corporations, the Dutch West India Company, the French Company of the West, the Royal African Company, and a host of private traders and privateers. They entered a society in which many people of European descent, although not slaves, were held in servitude of a variety of sorts. Almost immediately they began the work of integrating themselves into that society— taking familiar names, trading on their own, establishing families, accumulating property, and employing their knowledge of the law to advance themselves. They secured their freedom in remarkably high numbers. About one-fifth to one-quarter of the Charter Generation would gain their liberty.[28]

Little is known about these men and women with names— wonderfully telling names like Anthony Johnson of Virginia, Paulo d'Angola of New Amsterdam, and Francisco Menéndez of Saint

Augustine—that speak to the larger Atlantic world. Their history can be glimpsed through the life of another of their number—one Samba Bambara—who first appears in the historical record while working for the French Company of the West on the Senegal River in West Africa at the beginning of the eighteenth century. He is known because he disputed his pay and complained that his wife "dishonored" him. Working along the river, moving cargo—perhaps human cargo—from St. Louis to the interior, Samba Bambara rubbed shoulders with saltwater sailors of various European and African nationalities, traders from the interior, and the corporate bureaucrats who directed the Company of the West and the soldiers who protected the bureaucrats. He doubtless spoke the Creole language of the Atlantic along with his own language and a bit of French. Like others who followed his path, he became a cultural broker negotiating among the various peoples who had come together in the Atlantic.

Sometime in the 1720s, Samba Bambara became implicated in a slave insurrection in St. Louis, or perhaps he was merely accused of being involved. Nonetheless, he was enslaved and transported to Louisiana, a desultory society with slaves that stood at the fag end of the French empire. That in itself was a telling choice, for almost all the slaves leaving Senegal for the New World were going to Martinique or St. Domingue, colonies that were fast becoming the great sugar factories of the Atlantic world. But perhaps someone realized it was dangerous to send a man like Samba Bambara, a man who knew how the system worked, to revolutionary tinderboxes like Martinque or St. Domingue.

Doubtless Samba Bambara was not happy about his enslavement and exile, the forcible separation from everything and everyone he held dear. But once in New Orleans, he resumed his life almost without missing a beat. Within a decade, Samba Bambara—still a slave—was successively the overseer of the largest company-owned plantation in Louisiana and then chief interpreter in the Louisiana Superior Court.[29]

Samba Bambara's success suggests something about the unity of the Atlantic world. It reveals how New Orleans on the Mississippi River was not much different from St. Louis on the Senegal River, both ports filled with saltwater sailors from the Atlantic, native traders from the interior, European corporate bureaucrats, and settlers from all nations. New Orleans was, in short, a place in which a cultural broker like Samba Bambara could not only survive, but could also enjoy a modicum of success. The story of the Charter Generation was one of modest success. It certainly was different from the history of those who followed.

Its successors, the men and women who entered the mainland after the Plantation Revolution (in the Chesapeake with tobacco at the end of the seventeenth century, in the low country of Carolina with rice at the beginning of the eighteenth century, in the lower Mississippi Valley with sugar and cotton at the end of the eighteenth century and the beginning of the nineteenth) were not nearly as fortunate. Members of the Plantation Generation worked harder and died earlier. Their family life was truncated, and few men and women claimed ties of blood or marriage. They knew—and probably wanted to know—little about Christianity and European jurisprudence. They had but small opportunities to participate in independent exchange economies, and they rarely accumulated property. Most lived on large estates deep in the countryside, cut off from the larger Atlantic world. Few escaped slavery.

Their names reflected the contempt in which their owners held them. Most answered to some European diminutive—Jack and Sukey in the English colonies, Pedro and Francisca in places under Spanish rule, and Jean and Marie in the French dominions. As if to emphasize their inferiority, some were tagged with names more akin to barnyard animals. Others were designated with the names of some ancient deity or great personage like Hercules or Cato as a kind of cosmic jest: the most insignificant given the greatest of names. Whatever they were called, they rarely bore surnames, as their owners sought to obliterate marks of lineage and to deny adulthood. Such names suggest the anonymity of the Plantation Generation. The biographies of individual men and women, to the extent that they can be reconstructed, are thin to the point of invisibility. Less is known about these men and women than any other generation of American slaves.[30]

A similar change can be traced through the lives of men and women of African descent who came of age at the end of the eighteenth century amid the American, French, and Haitian revolutions. The Revolutionary Generation's history was also different from that of those who proceeded them, as they transformed themselves from Catos and Herculeses or Sukeyes and Phoebes to Richard Allens, Benjamin Bannakers, Phyllis Wheatleys, Prince Halls, and Daniel Cokers amid the demise of slavery in the Northern states and its expansion in the states of the Lower South.[31] As people of African descent took on new roles, the meaning of race again changed, as it would when nearly one million slaves—the Migration Generation—were forcibly dragged across the continent to Alabama, Mississippi, Louisiana, Arkansas, and Texas, transforming them as well as those left behind in the seaboard South.[32]

Understanding the ever-changing character of chattel bondage over the course of three centuries is part of a larger attempt to historicize the study of slavery. The purpose is to free slavery in the United States from the stereotypes that have bound it—stereotypes that lock it into the master narrative of the Civil War; stereotypes that connect it to the history of cotton, the Black Belt, and Afro-Christianity; stereotypes that fix it to contemporary notions of race; stereotypes that deny historical contingency and historical agency. In place of those stereotypes has arisen a history in which slavery was made by men and women on their own terms, if not exactly to their own liking. It is a history that reminds all that once something was different—that men and women made it so. From this perspective, slavery was not made but constantly remade.

Like all history, the new history of slavery is a critical reconstruction of past events based upon the belief that the past was
different. It is not simply that the past was slow and the present is fast
or that the eighteenth century was wooden and the twentieth century is plastic, or that once there were quills and now there are PCs,
but that the fundamental assumptions that governed men and
women in the past and the basic relationships they created were
different. The cliché is that the past is like a foreign country. Hence
it must be reconstructed on its own terms, with care not to confuse
it with the present or to weight it down with anachronisms. Lincoln
did not reside in the White House but the Presidential Mansion.
Slavery was not what white Southerners once called their "peculiar
institution," at least prior to the American Revolution.

While the past must be understood on its own terms, those terms
must be inclusive. However obscure or tainted, evidence must be
weighed and dispassionately considered. Whatever the convenience
of dividing the study of the past into its various components—
economic, social, political history, for example—the study of the
past must encompass all people. History is about relationships
that cannot be parsed. Universities may teach courses on workers,
women, and gays, but the history of workers cannot be separated
from the history of bosses, that of women from men, and that of
gays from straights, any more than one can distinguish "political
man" from "social man." Although historians rarely succeed, their
aim is to be universal and to connect all.

Thus the new history of slavery is part of a continuing debate
about the past, what happened, and what it means. It is an ongoing
debate because it is understood that the past can never be recovered in full. New evidence and new perspectives will inevitably shift interpretations. Likewise, it must be acknowledged that
there are some aspects of the past that will be known imperfectly
and, sadly, that there are some things that will never be known. By
definition, the reconstructed past is contested terrain. It proceeds

from great skepticism. Nothing is taken for granted. Everything is contingent. Everyone lied—at least as a presumption.

Memory of slavery in the United States is constructed on very different ground.[33] It rarely reaches back beyond the last generation of slavery—strategically eliminating the history of slavery in the North, along with the Charter Generation and much else. For the most part, it speaks to the experience of the last generation of slaves, those men and women who did grow cotton, reside in the Black Belt, and practice Christianity. Much of it was constructed in interviews recorded in the 1930s and 1940s under the auspices of the Federal Writer's Project, an agency of the New Deal charged with keeping unemployed artists and intellectuals off of the welfare rolls and committed to capturing the real American history—the people's history—not the history of the great magnates and moguls. It has since been amplified in the cinema, museums, monuments, living-history reenactments, as well as dozens of books, Web sites, and even battlefield recreations.[34]

The memory of slavery gives voice to the men and women who experienced slavery directly and tells two great stories. The first is the physical and psychological imposition that was at the heart of slavery, in all places and all times. These are stories of hideous, obscene violence: of mutilations, beatings, and rapes; of the forcible separation of husbands and wives, parents and children; of husbands forced to see their wives abused, and of wives forced to do unspeakable things. It is the story of power over liberty, of a people victimized and brutalized.

But there is a second theme. The story of slavery captured in the memories of those who lived it is not only a history of victimization and brutalization. If slavery was violence and imposition—if it was death—slavery was also life. Former slaves did not surrender to the imposition, physical and psychological. They refused to be dehumanized by dehumanizing treatment. On the narrowest of grounds and in the most difficult of circumstances, they created and sustained life in the form of families, churches, and associations of all kinds. These organizations—often clandestine and fugitive, fragile and unrecognized—created language, aesthetics, and philosophy that was expressed in story, music, dance, and cuisine. They produced leaders and ideologies that continue to inform American life. Indeed, the creative legacy of slavery is so great that it must be conceded that if slavery is the oppressive period of the American past, it may also be the most creative moment. It is impossible to imagine American culture without the creative legacy of slavery.

Giving voice to former slaves and their dual message of the dehumanizing force of slavery and the slaves' refusal to be dehumanized reveals how memory differs from history. For memory, unlike history, is not a skeptical reconstruction of the past. It is reflexive and unquestioned. It is absolute and instantaneous. It is not distant from the present but conjoined with today and contiguous with tomorrow. It speaks not to a desire to understand the whole or to include all in the story, but to personal understandings based upon the most intimate experiences learned in families, churches, and communities. It is conveyed through symbols and rituals, in knowing gestures, and often-repeated stories passed from grandparents who were too often ignored and kitchen-table banter that was barely heard over the din of business as usual. As such, memories are anything but tentative, distant, or contingent. They are immediate, intense, and emotive. They evoke not skepticism, but demand acceptance and commitment. They command loyalty, not controversy. Memories are not debated (except in the most trivial sense), they are embraced. They are, after all, about us.

- Memories are the picture of the slave ship *Brooks*, with its cargo of tightly packed men and women stuffed spoonlike into its hull, which has recently appeared on posters in college dorms and on T-shirts, often emblazoned with the words, "Never forget."[35]
- Memories are Thomas Jefferson's relationship with Sally Hemings and the refusal to recognize paternity, personal but also national.[36]
- Memories are the debates about naming high schools after Denmark Vesey, Nat Turner, and the slave rebel Gabriel and about the

removing of the names of Robert E. Lee, Stonewall Jackson, and Jefferson Davis—and, of course, the Confederate flag.[37]

If history is skeptical, contested, and universal, memory is certain, incontestable, and personal. If, at its best, history is a dispassionate weighing of all the evidence, memory is a selective recall of a piece of the past that makes no pretense of being universal. If the history of slavery speaks to the world transformed, the memory of slavery addresses what was done to my people, my family, me. For former slaves, it reiterates that lives lost and mutilated should not be forgotten. A rich legacy was created at great cost and homage must be paid to those who paid the price. It demands that we root out the deniers, unmask the disassemblers, and remind those who would forget. Never forget!

This may be true enough, but such a formulation speaks against the skeptical, critical, and all-inclusive inspection of the past that is at the heart of the historical enterprise. For former slaves, the study of slavery is not something that can be viewed dispassionately, questioned, inspected, and debated. They must be recognized, embraced, and celebrated. For the reality of slavery was absolute and undeniable. They, after all, were there.

But, if this is so, what of slavery's history, the world of the Charter Generation: of Samba Bambara, Paulo d'Angola, Francisco Menéndez? What of the members of the Plantation Generation whose names were taken from them and hidden from us? And what of Richard Allen, Benjamin Bannaker, Prince Hall, and Phyllis Wheatley of the Revolutionary Generation, who recovered their names and built African American life on new terrain? Indeed, what of the Migration Generation, who had to reconstruct their lives in the Black Belt and who embraced a church their fathers and mothers had denied? And what of the Freedom Generation whose voices would carry slavery's diverse memories into the twentieth and then the twenty-first centuries? They too were there.

What of slavery's history? It is a history that was constructed not only from slaves' African descent but also from their American experience, the unique experience that derived from the diverse landscapes upon which they lived, economies in which they worked, and societies in which they were enmeshed. It is a history that is derived from battles that were won and lost and that, in the process, created identities that were made and remade. If the memory of slavery is fixed and undeniable, the history is contingent and endlessly debatable. How many slaves crossed the Atlantic? What was the nature of the slave family? Why were there so few slave rebellions, or so many? When did slaves become Christians, and what did Christianity mean? These matters must be debatable, because to deny the debate is to remove slaves from history, mummify them and separate them from the real world. It too denies the undeniable.

History and memory speak to the subject of slavery and the long experience of people of African descent in America, but they speak in different tongues. These different tongues each reflect the manner in which the subject of slavery has been parsed. They also reflect how such division denies the contemporary impact of slavery only to revivify it on demand to make the memory of slavery conform to contemporary political purposes.

Put the matter to this point. If memory were denied—if history were allowed to trump memory—the past would not be relevant to twenty-first-century Americans either black or white. Everything they know and value—their politics, the kind of world they live in, the kind of world they would like to build—would lack the visceral attachment and incentive that memory instills. But if history were denied——if memory were allowed to trump history—the past would become a mere shadow of the present with no real purpose other than to provide wish fulfillment or at best a myth with footnotes. It may be a source of great satisfaction to some, but of little value beyond assertion.

Slavery lives—and will continue to live—in both history and memory. But the time has come to put the two together, to join history and memory, to embrace slavery's complex history, to accept the force of slavery's memory, and thereby elevate both. For only by testing memory against history can a sense of a collective past be sustained. Perhaps by incorporating slavery's memory into slavery's history—and vice versa—Americans, white and black, can have a past that is both memorable and—at last—past.

2

The Quest for Freedom: Runaway Slaves and the Plantation South

JOHN HOPE FRANKLIN
and LOREN SCHWENINGER

J ANE WAS YESTERDAY afternoon about six o'clock arrested," Charles Colcock Jones, Jr., of Savannah began in a letter to his father on the first day of October 1856; "she is now in confinement in Wright the broker's yard." Owned by cotton planter Charles C. Jones, Sr., of Liberty County, Georgia, Jane had been in Savannah more than a month before being discovered. She had passed herself off as a slave from the upcountry who was permitted to hire her own time, and she had found employment at $6.50 a week doing housework.

This was not the first time Jane had been arrested as a runaway. Indeed, by age eighteen, wearing "fine ear- and finger-rings," the corpulent, garrulous, self-confident black woman had traversed the thirty miles from Jones's plantation to the city on many occasions, so many that she knew the route by heart: north to the Great Ogeechee River, stealing a boat and crossing the river, then wending her way around ponds, creeks, and drainage canals to the forests of live oaks and cypress swamps, and on to the Savannah road. On previous trips, she had found passage on coastal vessels, making part of the journey in a fish-hook fashion to the mouth of the Savannah River, and thence to the city. Late summer was not a good time to run, as the daytime heat lingered and the nights remained stiflingly hot. But the weather seemed to make little difference to Jane.

How should the father and son deal with the problem? Should they attempt to reason with Jane about the self-destructive nature of her behavior? Should they administer corporal punishment? Should they sell her away from her mother, father, brothers, and sister? In addition, should they prosecute the woman who had hired Jane? With regard to the latter, the son explained, "There are, you may say, hundreds of Negroes in this city who go about from house to house—some carpenters, some house servants, etc.—who never see their masters except at pay day, live out of their yards, hire themselves without written permit." This was of course "very wrong," he wrote, but "the less said and done in cases of this kind the better."

Accepting his son's advice, the father anguished about the various other alternatives. A deeply religious and pious man, devoted to improving the spiritual well-being of his slaves, Jones weighed the question with great care. In the end, however, he declared, "We have had trouble enough, and I wish to have no more." He would sell Jane as soon as possible. Unlike many slaveholders, who sought to maximize profits, he instructed his son to sell Jane, her mother, age forty-seven, her father, age forty-five, and her four siblings as one group. Another field hand would also be disposed of at the same time and the eight placed on the market in Savannah should bring $6,700, including $900 for Jane, who was advertised as a "House servant, good seamstress, and field hand."

Weeks passed, however, and the slaves remained unsold. An offer of $4,200 was made by George Harrison, "a gentleman of high respectability" who would "make a good master," but it was rejected as being too low. Meanwhile, Jones was paying $10.50

per week to maintain the slaves in Savannah, and as costs mounted, he and his son grew apprehensive. Finally, about two months after Jane had been arrested, the son sold the slaves for $4,500, far less than anticipated. The consolation was that the purchaser, claiming to be from Macon, was a planter who promised to treat the family well and keep them together. "They have been sold as we desired," the father wrote with relief. More money might have been made, but they were kept together. "Conscience is better than money."[1]

The events surrounding Jane's escape, capture, and subsequent sale occurred many thousands of times as slavery spread across the South during the decades following the American Revolution. An examination of runaway slaves between 1790 and 1860 reveals how a significant number of slaves challenged the system, and how the great majority of them struggled to attain their freedom even if they failed. The price they paid for their unwillingness to submit was obviously enormous.

The most common form of absconding was not actually running away at all, but what might be termed truancy, absenteeism, and in some cases, lying out. The terms are imprecise as they were used to describe a broad range of resistance—from slaves staying out a few days and coming back on their own accord to joining runaway gangs and causing havoc by pillage and looting. Generally, those who left for short periods stayed in the vicinity of the plantation and returned on their own accord. Those who left for a few nights to be with loved ones were not technically runaways. At times, truants were hunted as such, and the line was sometimes blurred. After hiding in the woods, one Louisiana slave sent her child back to the plantation. The overseer noted that he now believed she (and several others with her) were "only laying out," and his previous belief that she had run away was "groundless."[2]

Absenteeism was so common that most masters attempted to deal with it by inflicting mild punishments or ignoring it altogether. The great majority of slaves who sneaked away from their farms and plantations overnight or for a few days had specific destinations in mind, namely to visit their wives, husbands, sons, daughters, other family members, and friends. Others left to go hunting or fishing, traveled into towns, go to dances or religious meetings, secretly meet members of the opposite sex, or visit the back rooms of grocery stores to drink and play cards. Sometimes absentees sought to gain certain concessions from their owners— better clothing, rations, working conditions, housing, visitation privileges—but such efforts were rare, and rarer still were the occasions when they were successful. Why should owners negotiate with their own property? The movement of slaves from one plantation to another or into town without permission was not a matter of public concern or noted in newspapers. Indeed, most slave owners, like Charles C. Jones, Jr., in Savannah, felt it better to keep such matters quiet unless such movements posed a threat.

Despite its common occurrence, leaving without permission could pose a danger for slaves. Those caught trying to sneak away might face reprisals, and those who remained away too long might test their owners' patience. Worse still, if a slave were discovered on someone else's property, hiding in the slave quarters, that could be serious indeed. In Oglethorpe County, Georgia, in 1850, the slave Henry was discovered early one morning lying on his wife's bed in the kitchen on the plantation where she was a slave. The overseer, Willis Jones, ordered him to "rise and cross his hands," but Henry refused and, being a much larger man, threw the overseer against the wall. "It was 2 O'clock A.M.," the owner of the plantation, Moses Wright, later testified in a civil suit, "and I was sound asleep." Running to assist the overseer he found them clenched. Wright grabbed Henry from behind, took a rope from the overseer's pocket, and the two white men tied Henry's hands and "bucked him." The overseer then administered seventy-five lashes with a cowhide whip well laid on for resisting, and another thirty or forty stripes "for intruding on the Premises contrary to orders."[3]

Staying away from the plantation for longer periods—weeks sometimes months—was also a common practice. Those who stayed in the same vicinity of their owners' farm or plantation were said to be "lying out." This could range from leaving for short periods with every intention of returning to leaving for longer periods and setting up camps in remote back sections. Lying out tested an owner's patience to a much greater degree than did mere truancy and was usually dealt with more harshly. Slaves who laid out often lived by fishing, hunting, stealing, trading, and looting. They encamped near towns and cities, along rivers and streams, or in dense forests and swamps. They stayed alone, in small groups, and occasionally in large bands. Sometimes they stayed near relatives or friends, even hid in quarters on neighboring plantations.

Indeed, there were few sections of the South where farmers did not complain about blacks in their vicinity who were "lurking about near the plantations" and doing "mischief." Sometimes they moved back and forth in broad daylight, unafraid of being seen by whites and other slaves. One Lenoir County, North Carolina, slave owner said in 1818 that his outlying slave had been seen frequently roaming about "my own neighborhood" carrying a gun "and other weapons for defense." If anyone would pay him $600, he would sell the black man "as he runs."[4]

Even under the best of circumstances those remaining nearby confronted many obstacles. Living conditions could be harsh, with inadequate food, water, shelter, and clothing. Often the weather—stifling heat, incessant rains, and in the border states, frigid cold—was as much a problem as finding food. Over the years, the increasing density of settlement, improvements in communication, and the rising frequency of patrols created additional problems. Struggling against a variety of difficulties, a number of outlying slaves returned on their own.

Few absconders remained permanently at large. Slaves who remained in the neighborhood for extended periods were usually among the most ingenious, intelligent, and fearless. They maintained contacts with friends or relatives on plantations who provided them with food, clothing, shelter, and information. Sometimes slaves traded stolen goods with merchants and other whites or took pilfered items into towns and cities to sell. Familiar with the area, they would appear for brief periods, move about, and disappear. In Charleston District, South Carolina, a group of about a dozen slaves—including three brothers and a married couple with children—hid out in the densely wooded areas around their owners' plantations. They moved about, maintaining several base camps, and passed frequently between plantations. They also communicated with and visited town slaves. They moved in and out of slave quarters so freely and frequently that one planter, unable to recognize his own chattel, issued identification cards to his slaves, cards describing the bearer and to be renewed weekly.[5]

Sometimes outlying slaves gathered together in bands and wreaked havoc on farms and plantations. Living in isolated, heavily wooded, or swampy areas, some of these groups maintained their cohesiveness for several years, a few for more than a generation. Most, however, found it difficult to sustain themselves living in only one location. Members of fugitive gangs made forays into populated farming areas for food, clothing, livestock, and trading items. Sometimes they bartered with free blacks, plantation slaves, non-slaveholding whites, and in a few instances, white outlaws joined the outlying gangs, though this was rare. In virtually every Southern state, especially in areas having dense black populations, there were small bands of outlying slaves. The largest bodies of maroons, as they were sometimes called, numbered only a few hundred. Exceptions to this were those in the Great Dismal Swamp between North Carolina and Virginia, which numbered several thousand, and the runaways who joined the Seminole Indians in the Everglades of Florida.

Though ephemeral in nature, runaway gangs were a constant source of fear and anxiety for whites.[6] Such was the case in Onslow County, North Carolina, where, in the summer of 1821, an insurrection of "outlawed and runaway Slaves and free Negroes" broke out. Located between the White Oak and the New rivers in the eastern portion of the state, Onslow's long estuaries and dense forests provided good cover. The outlying slaves "daily increased in strength and numbers," William L. Hill, head of a militia unit, wrote. Their bold acts of defiance became so alarming that no inhabitant felt safe, in person or property, from their "plunder, rapine, and devastation." Reports circulated about "violence and depredations" against the "persons and property of defenseless and unprotected families." The slaves were well armed, cunning, and bold, Hill said. They ravaged farms—burning houses, breaking into stores, and raping white women. Riding through "Woods, Swamps & Marshes," it took Hill's two-hundred-man militia twenty-six days to subdue the "Outlaws."[7]

The great majority of runaways, however, was not involved in insurrections. Rather, they ran away alone and sought to distance themselves as much as possible from their owners. On October 25, 1816, William W. Bell, a North Carolina farmer, placed a notice in the *North Carolina Minerva and Raleigh Advertiser* about his runaway slave. Explaining that he had purchased Frank from John Patterson of Matthews County, Virginia, Bell wrote:

RUNAWAY, from the Subscriber, on Friday Evening last, Near Enfield Court House, a NEGRO MAN, named FRANK, pretty stout, one strait scar on his cheek passing from the under part of the ear towards the corner of the mouth, of a common dark color, something of a flat nose, a short, round chin, and a down look, about 26 or 27 years of age. Had on, brown yarn homespun Pantaloons, striped homespun waistcoat, and a white yarn roundabout. TWENTY-FIVE DOLLARS reward will be given *for lodging* said runaway in any gaol in this state or TWENTY DOLLARS if in any gaol out of the state.[8]

Forty-one years later, in the fall of 1857, a South Carolina planter, E. M. Royall, published a similar notice in the *Charleston Mercury*:

TWENTY-FIVE DOLLARS REWARD.—Ranaway from the subscriber's plantation, in Christ Church Parish, his Negro Man TONEY. Said fellow is about 5 feet 6 inches in height; stoutly built, is very black, has a broad, full face, black eyes, and when he laughs, shows a very white set of teeth. The above reward will be paid for his apprehension and delivery to the Work House in Charleston, or to the subscriber on his place.[9]

In size, build, color, gender, age, attire, reward, probable occupation, and personality—at least as perceived by whites—Frank and Toney fit the profile of typical runaway slaves. The largest segment of the runaway army included strong, young field hands in their late teens and twenties. The two advertisements also demonstrate the continuity that existed among typical runaways from one generation to the next.

A statistical analysis of more than two thousand slaves advertised in newspapers in five states (Virginia, North Carolina, South Carolina, Tennessee, and Louisiana) during two time periods—early, or 1790–1816, and late, or 1838–1860—reveals that Frank and Toney were indeed representative.[10] Four out of five runaways among those sought were male, and three out of four among them were between the ages of thirteen and twenty-nine. Young men ran away in greater numbers because often they had not yet married, or, if they had married, had not yet begun a family. Those who married sometimes took their families with them, but in most cases, they were forced to leave wives and children behind. Young men also ran away more often because they were more willing to defy overseers and owners. Once away from the plantation, they were better able to defend themselves and resist capture.

If the typical runaway was a young male field hand, runaways also included a range of other slaves, black and mulatto, female and male, skilled and unskilled, urban and rural, young and old, healthy and infirm. They escaped from plantations, farms, urban residences, job sites, and river boats. Indeed, despite the norm, runaways were a diverse lot, and judging from their comments, slave owners seemed unable to predict who might abscond. Nathan, a Tennessee slave, had become a habitual runaway before reaching his tenth birthday, while one South Carolina man described a captured fugitive as being "about eighty years old."[11]

Although the spectacular escapes depicted in slave narratives and abolitionist literature were not without basis in fact, the great majority of runaways absconded neither dramatically nor successfully. Rather, they sneaked off at night, on Saturday afternoon or Sunday, or during holidays. They stowed away on sailing vessels and steamboats, crawled into the backs of wagons, concealed themselves in barns, outbuildings, or abandoned houses. They camped out in the woods and swamps. A few rode off on their owners' horses, or with their owners' wagons. By the 1840s and 1850s, some slipped aboard trains or purchased railroad tickets, posing as free persons of color.[12]

Their reasons for running away were as varied as their methods of escape. Of course, the desire for freedom was fundamental, but a slave's departure was usually precipitated by some grievance, fear, or conflict. The causes of dissatisfaction that could prompt such a response seem infinite: oppressive working conditions; inadequate food; scant clothing; bad housing; prohibitions on spousal visits; fear of being sold; displeasure with a new master; dissatisfaction with hiring arrangements; ill treatment; excessive punishment.

The plantation "crimes" that sent slaves running—murder, assault, arson, poisoning, rape, pillage, burglary, theft—were frequent occurrences. Runaways also frequently had participated in a variety of clandestine economic activities, especially the bartering, trading, buying, and selling of stolen goods. These overt and covert acts of resistance brought swift, often brutal, responses from owners or overseers. Malingering, lying out, and "accidental" destruction of livestock and machinery might be overlooked. Open defiance was different. For slaves and masters alike, it was a matter of grave concern.

Most slaves understood the potential consequences of assaulting a white person. In the period following the American Revolution, it could mean summary execution. Even later, when property laws offered more protection to slave owners, extreme punishment was common. What is surprising is the persistence of violence on the plantation. Such incidents often went unreported. Masters did not wish to admit a failure in governing their human property, and rumors that a slave was aggressive or belligerent diminished the slave's monetary value. But the popular myth that "slaves are more generally good tempered than other people" is not supported by the evidence. Most of the violence was spontaneous, and most of it was directed against whites—owners, members of their families, overseers—although it could also be directed against fellow slaves.

Among the many causes of slaves running away, perhaps none was more pervasive than seeking to reunite with family members. Slaves ran to neighboring plantations to be with husbands or wives. They ran to search for mothers and fathers. And all too often they ran, in vain, to retrieve their children. It was especially wrenching for youngsters to be torn away from parents or to see their parents sent away. Usually they were sold off and never saw members of their families again. It is hard to exaggerate the trauma of being forever separated from kith and kin.

Most slaves were sold at one time or another during their life-time, and often it was when they were young and would bring the highest price. Seldom were families sold together in units of father, mother, and children. The separation of family members was commonplace after 1820. As whites poured into the Tennessee and Mississippi river valleys, demand for young male slaves grew dramatically. In the Louisiana sugar parishes, 70 percent of the slaves purchased were male, many bought from traders from the upper states who scoured the countryside looking for young black men. In the Upper South, forcible separations probably destroyed one out of three first marriages, and roughly one out of three slave children under age fifteen was separated from one or both parents.[13]

As the prices brought by slaves rose in the West and the profits from the interstate trade increased during the late antebellum era, increasing numbers of women and young children were swept into the domestic slave trade. They were bought at private sales, auctions, and estate sales, then transported to the West where they were sold at a substantial profit. Although many owners denied they would ever engage in such a practice, speculation in black youngsters was not uncommon. "What can be had for two (2) girls number one about seven (7) the other nine[?]" one Richmond slave trader asked. "I bought today a likely girl, I suppose she is 12 year[s] old, 4 ft 10 inches high," he added, asking, "Do you think it a good time to sell[?] If so I will send her in."[14] A second trader wrote to the same firm inquiring if there was "anything doing in your negro Markette." He wanted to know what he could get for "a good girl 13 yrs old, one 12 yrs old, and a boy 10 yrs old, or wheather [sic] there wd be any certainty of my selling them at all."[15] The buying and selling of black children ages seven through thirteen bore witness to the breaking up of families.

As a result, runaways set out in a variety of directions, sometimes deeper into the South where planters had an insatiable appetite for fresh workers. "There is little doubt that Jim has gone to the Southward," explained a planter on the Cooper River in South Carolina in 1831 concerning his runaway carpenter who had been missing for six months. Jim recently had been sold away from the Colleton District and would no doubt return to that area.[16]

Slaves living in the Lower Mississippi River valley or in Mississippi and Alabama were more likely to run south and west than north. The stream of runaways moving from Natchitoches, Rapides, Pointe Coupee, East and West Feliciana, and Baton Rouge parishes in Louisiana and Adams, Jefferson, and Wilkinson counties in Mississippi, south to New Orleans was continuous. "Ranaway from the subscriber's plantation, in the parish of Natchitoches," one typical notice read, describing William Chambery. He was about twenty years old and "well constituted."[17] The planter sought not only Chambery, but also "his negro wench Louisa," "negro wench Eliza," and a black man, Henry Price. They were, he said, heading down the Cane, Red, and Mississippi rivers, to New Orleans.[18]

Thus, for many runaways the direction was dictated by expectation of a place where they might find loved ones, obtain assistance, secure employment, or mix with other slaves or free blacks. Some simply set out in a direction they felt they would least likely be pursued. Others followed the course of a river or boarded a vessel not knowing its destination. A few did not know where to go. Ignorance of geography was common among whites and blacks, and slaves knew only what they had observed after being taken from one location to another or what they had been told by others. Some had never traveled beyond their owners' plantation. A Tennessee fugitive who made it to Ohio recalled that prior to running away he had never ventured more than seventeen miles from his owner's farm.[19]

The dream of freedom in the North or Canada—the so-called Promised Land—went unfulfilled for the vast majority of runaways. Those who absconded northward from plantations along the coast of South Carolina and Georgia, the Black Belt of Alabama, the Mississippi Delta, or sugar parishes of Louisiana faced a trek of hundreds of miles through uncharted and largely unknown terrain. Even their counterparts in the upper states confronted numerous obstacles to making it to free territory. A few were able to find assistance from conductors of the Underground Railroad, Quakers, or antislavery whites. And a few others, traveling at night or hiding aboard sailing vessels and steamboats, made it to the North. But the chances of making it to New Jersey, Pennsylvania, or across the Ohio River were remote.

Even residency in the border state of Maryland, in close proximity to freedom, did not ensure success. Most who lived in the Chesapeake region probably ended up like Willis Burgess, an estate slave hired out by the executor. Absconding from his employer in Anne Arundel County in 1836, Burgess headed northwest into Baltimore County, moved swiftly along the road to Hanover, and then turned toward his destination: York, Pennsylvania. Late that same night, however, he was captured and put in the Baltimore city jail. After the episode, the executor who hired Burgess out deemed it "most prudent" to sell him, and a few days later, Burgess was placed on the auction block.[20]

The chances of remaining at large were perhaps best for those who, like Jane, ran away to towns and cities. As with runaways who remained near the plantation, those who ran to urban areas were often apprehended. But cities offered unique opportunities. By the early 1800s, slave hiring and self-hire had grown to such an extent that in some cities there were hundreds, even thousands, of hired bondsmen and bondswomen. As a consequence, runaways could pose as self-hired slaves, hide their identities, create new ones, live with their relatives—slave and free—and mingle with other blacks. They might be accosted and questioned, but control was less intrusive than in the country, where black strangers were scrutinized and often arrested. It was little wonder that the streets of Southern cities—teeming with carts, buggies, wagons, drays, livestock, mules, horses, and pedestrians—beckoned to runaway slaves.

To deal with the problem of runaways, every Southern state enacted an extensive set of laws. While differing slightly from state to state, the codes and the civil and criminal cases that evolved were similar in defining the runaways, how they should be apprehended, and what the consequences would be. Any slave "who shall be found more than twenty miles distant from the plantation, tenement, or other place where such slave is employed or required to be by his owner, overseer or employer, without a written pass or permission" was a runaway, an 1839 Arkansas statute said, mirroring those in other states. Any white person could apprehend the slave and turn him or her over to a justice of the peace. The apprehender would receive reimbursement from the county for the mileage he had traveled and was eligible for a fifteen-dollar reward. The county sheriff was instructed to advertise the captured slave, describing him or her by name, physical appearance, wearing apparel, and name of owner. If the runaway went unclaimed for twelve months, the sheriff was instructed to advertise and sell the slave at the courthouse to the highest bidder. Owners could reclaim their property at any time before the auction or designate others to do so.[21]

The laws also established patrols, ranging in size from small groups of two or three men to larger units of several dozen. They were organized in military fashion, with captains, sergeants, and patrollers (privates); and they had legal authority to search virtually anywhere for runaways. In times of crises, they could hold appointment through "executive authority," as in Virginia in 1808 when special patrols were formed to put down a rumored slave insurrection. As one patroller said, they were instructed to search "the negro cabins, & take every thing which we found in them, which bore a hostile aspect, such as powder, shot &c." They were further told to "apprehend every negro whom we found from his home; & if he made any resistance, or ran from us, to fire on him immediately, unless he could be stopped by other means." In most areas with large black populations, patrols frequently roamed across the countryside during the nighttime hours to flush out runaways.[22]

More effective than patrols in apprehending runaways were "professional" slave catchers, men who specialized in tracking and capturing missing slaves. They sometimes owned or could secure dogs and were willing to expend substantial effort to find their prey. Slave catchers were hired by planters who could not spare their overseers or other employees to go on frequent expeditions that could last for days or weeks. Charging by the day and mile, these men were often illiterate, nonslaveholding whites who could earn what was for them a sizeable sum—ten to fifty dollars—for bringing in a runaway. Typical of this group was Edward King of Concordia Parish, Louisiana, who in 1831 charged six cents a mile and two dollars a day, plus expenses.[23] One popular method of tracking slaves, especially during the 1840s and 1850s, was to use highly trained "Negro dogs." Frederick Law Olmsted observed that no particular breed was required for the hunt—bloodhounds, foxhounds, bulldogs, Scotch staghounds, curs—because slave hunters and planters had a method of training each breed to be effective. The dogs were locked up and "never allowed to see a negro except while training to catch him." They were given the scent of a black man or woman's shoe or article of clothing and taught to follow the scent. Slaves were sent out as trainees and the dogs were given meat as a reward for treeing them.[24] Despite Olmsted's observations, specially bred bloodhounds were clearly the dogs of choice. Louisiana slave owner and presidential candidate Zachary Taylor imported hounds from the Caribbean that were trained to chase slaves. The dogs were fierce hunters and if not restrained at the end of the chase, they would tear their quarry to pieces.[25]

For slaves who were difficult to find or remained out for weeks or months, owners sometimes offered rewards. Describing their slaves in newspapers or on printed handbills, owners promised to pay travel expenses, jail fees, and other costs. The number of such notices represented only a tiny fraction of the total number of runaways, but advertisements for slaves who had "eloped" were ubiquitous. They could be found in "nearly every court-house, tavern, and post-office," one observer said. Indeed, it would have been difficult to travel any distance or read any newspaper, even in sections far removed from the great plantation regions, without being reminded that there were runaway slaves "lurking about."[26]

Seeking the return of their property, masters and overseers wrote tens of thousands of these notices, varying from a few lines to lengthy and detailed paragraphs. The handbills and newspaper advertisements were objective and accurate in describing the demeanor, dress, speech, character, abilities, background, possible destination, and mental abilities of runaway slaves. To falsify a notice, of course, would be self-defeating. It is also noteworthy that the advertisements are virtually free of racial stereotypes. As one master said, his slave was "quick spoken" and a "sharp looking fellow," and another described his slave as not only "very smart" but "very plausible."[27] Runaways were described as handsome, intelligent, and articulate; as artful, conniving, and subtle; as deceptive, cunning, and ruthless. Sampson, a Louisiana slave who worked on a steamboat, was described as "a good looking negro and very intelligent."[28] The New Orleans "American negro" Isaac was "large and strongly built," with a handsome face and nonchalant air.[29]

Most owners offered very modest rewards for the return of their slave property. In the statistical overview previously mentioned, owners who placed notices during the early period offered an average bounty of fifteen dollars, and in the later period only twenty-five dollars. There were variations between states, with an average of eighteen dollars in Virginia during the early years compared with nine dollars in South Carolina. The average in Tennessee during the later years stood at thirty-two dollars compared with fourteen dollars in North Carolina. Moreover, these averages include a significant percentage (between one-fourth and one-fifth) offering no remuneration. But even excluding those who failed to promise payment, the average reward offered by slaveholders was less than 10 percent of a runaway's value. Indeed, as the prices of slaves increased, the average reward actually declined in relation to what slaves were bringing on the auction block. That this was the case tells us a great deal about the hunters and the hunted in the slave system. Rewards as a relation to slave value declined over time because owners were served by an increasingly sophisticated system for the recovery of their property.

While the number of advertisements for runaways rose dramatically during the 1840s and 1850s, one gets the clear impression that the number of runaways for whom there was no advertisement rose even more. Absconders were so common that it was indeed impossible to advertise for even a small percentage of those who made off. Owners had to consider legal costs, transportation charges, and jail fees in addition to a reward. Newspapers were often in distant towns and cities, and the trail could be cold by the time an ad appeared. In view of the various means at their disposal for recovering runaways—patrols, slave catchers, hiring agents, communication with other planters, black spies, white reward seekers—it is not surprising that masters offered modest rewards.

Contemporary estimates of the number of slaves who ran away varied considerably. J. D. B. De Bow, author of *A Compendium of the Seventh Census*, claimed that the number was minuscule. As superintendent of the census, De Bow, who came from New Orleans, explained that census marshals in 1850 had asked every slave owner in the region how many bondsmen and bondswomen had run away during the previous year and remained at large.[30] De Bow reported that only 1,011 slaves out of 3.2 million had run away and were still at large. In his view, this was strong evidence that slaves were happy and content.[31]

The questions census takers asked of slave owners not only produced flawed results, but failed even to hint at the magnitude of the problem. Although it will never be known exactly how many slaves absconded during any given year, Frederick Law Olmsted discovered as he toured the South during the 1850s that on virtually every large or medium-sized plantation he visited masters complained about runaways. Even in sections of the Lower South where blacks had "no prospect of finding shelter within hundreds of miles, or of long avoiding recapture and severe punishment, many slaves had a habit of frequently making efforts to escape temporarily from their ordinary condition of subjection." Throughout the Southern states, Olmsted concluded, "slaves are accustomed to 'run away.'"[32]

Olmsted was essentially correct. It was a rare planter among those who owned twenty or more slaves who could boast that none of his or her slaves had ever run off. Indeed, many confronted the problem at least once or twice a year, and a few struggled to control a plague of runaways. Nor was it uncommon for blacks to flee from slaveholders who owned fewer than twenty slaves. In

1860, there were about three hundred eighty-five thousand slave owners in the South, of whom about forty-six thousand were planters. If only half of all planters experienced a single runaway in a year, and if only 10 or 15 percent of other slaveholders faced the same problem (both extremely conservative estimates) the number of runaways annually would exceed fifty thousand. Add to this the number of slaves who ran away two, three, and more times in a year, and it becomes clear that Olmsted's impressionistic observation was far more accurate than the "scientific" data provided in the United States Census.

Despite this epidemic of runaways, the vast majority of slave owners, from middling farmers to the great planters—including Jane's owner, Charles C. Jones, Sr.— considered themselves kind, God-fearing, humane masters. Admittedly it was sometimes necessary to sell black children away from parents, wives away from husbands, and older slaves away from friends and kin. It was also necessary to correct recalcitrant slaves, as one would discipline one's own children. However, these actions were done not out of malice or caprice but out of necessity. These were the painful duties in an institution that had helped create the greatest civilization the world had ever known.

Why, then, did so many slaves run away? Owners denied it was because of poor treatment. They claimed to deal with their slaves in a "uniformly kind and considerate" manner or treated them "more like a child than a Servant," as George Washington said when one of his slaves made off.[33] As time passed, and the problem persisted, quite a few slave owners believed that it might be attributable to some disease, a "monomania," as one observer said, "to which the negro race is peculiarly subject."[34]

Dr. Samuel Cartwright, a prominent New Orleans physician, offered a diagnosis. In an article published in De Bow's Review in 1851, Cartwright explained that many slaves suffered from "DRAPETOMANIA, OR THE DISEASE CAUSING NEGROES TO RUN AWAY." The name was derived from the Greek δραπέγης (runaway slave) and μανια (mad or crazy). Absconding from service was "as much a disease of the mind," Cartwright wrote, "as any other species of mental alienation."[35]

Charles Colcock Jones and his son would certainly have applied the "mental alienation" theory to Jane, a habitual runaway. Whatever motives they might have imputed to her, however, they were surprised and shocked to learn of her fate. Eight months after Jane ran away, the father wrote to the son again about his former slave. "Here seems to be deception—a wheel within a wheel!" The planter from Macon who promised to keep the family together was in fact a slave trader who took them to the auction block in New Orleans. Now, Jones had received word about the "death of poor Jane! How soon and unexpectedly has she been cut off," he anguished, "the cause of all that has been done! Would that she had lived and died at home in peace with God and with the world! I have long prayed for those people many, many, very many times. I wish them well."[36]

Neither Jones's prayers nor his best wishes were a consolation to those slaves who were awaiting sale, nor to the intransigent Jane, who simply could not remain enslaved.

3

"Tradition Informs Us": African Americans' Construction of Memory in the Antebellum North

SCOTT HANCOCK

SOMETIME AFTER the American Revolution, John Hancock presented a silk flag to a unique company of soldiers in recognition of their service. Like other soldiers, they had risked their lives. Their uniqueness stemmed not from the nature of their service but from the nature of their being. These soldiers were black. Some were likely former slaves, representing the hopes of thousands and crowning the ideals of the country—or at least, decades later, that is how they would be remembered, as this cherished flag and the stories it represented passed down to succeeding generations.

In the antebellum United States, free black Northerners responded to challenges to their citizenship by arguing that they belonged in and to the United States. African Americans evoked their ancestors' service to the country as soldiers and sailors during war, and as diligent, law-abiding workers during peace. Black memory did not rely on how other Americans remembered the Revolutionary past, but built on a kind of oral tradition maintained within Northern black communities. Though African American oral tradition had evolved in distinct ways from its African roots, much of the purpose remained the same. Storytelling, for black people, was performance—not just for entertainment, but also for political, educational, social, moral, and cultural ends. Telling the stories of one's people shaped identity, and often reinforced or even demanded a certain social and political standing. Who you were depended on who you had been.[1]

Oral traditions differ from oral histories. Stories told by an eyewitness constitute an oral history. Oral traditions do the same, though the story is often not told by the participant and may even be several generations removed from the initial experience. And oral traditions literally do more. They are public performances with ritual and purpose. The stories may vary in degrees of veracity. This does not mean they are filled with falsehoods and inaccuracies; it is more a question of what gets included, what gets emphasized, and what gets left out. The oral traditions black Northerners engaged in were relatively young—a mere half-century old or so— and therefore were more likely to have been fairly accurate. Typically, succeeding generations tended to keep only what was significant for their present. Regardless of accuracy, when stories were performed, participants "reconstruct and perpetuate the history of a mythic past in order to better understand both that past and [their] own time in a historic and ritual continuum." "Mythic" past does not mean that what is contained is factually incorrect, but it is often factually incomplete, and it therefore creates or shapes a group's perceptions of the past—of their history. Those perceptions in turn form a group's collective memory.[2]

African American oral traditions helped build memory by cultivating stories and by pruning any blemishes that might mar the image free black Northerners sought to create. This essay examines the construction of memory maintained in oral traditions and pushed into print for the purpose of attempting to secure African Americans' role in the birth, maintenance, and future of a republic that was unsure of their place in it. This countered the dominant national narrative, which excluded the black role in its founding and progress. Black memory played a careful game and played it well. Intentionally and unintentionally, African Americans crafted a memory that protested their exclusion from the dominant narrative while simultaneously critiquing that narrative. When an individual or group is excluded from social or cultural memory, it can be "tantamount to both social extinction and deprivation of identity" in relation to larger society.[3] Black Northerners effectively combated that, but did so in part by also practicing their own form of exclusion. They essentially extinguished the experiences of select groups of eighteenth-century slaves in order to allow nineteenth-century freed people to identify themselves as patriotic Americans.

Scant attention has been paid to creation of black memory before the Civil War. Ralph Ellison noted that "Negro American consciousness is not a product... of a will to historical forgetfulness." African Americans formed an identity—a sense of what it meant to be African American—in part through determined remembrance in the face of a society that strived mightily to forget them and their role in America's past. Remembering their role began soon after the country's founding. But, like most other social groups, part of that remembrance—the creation of a collective black memory—did indeed involve a will to forget.[4]

Black memory competed with white collective memory by acknowledging a black role and by highlighting the country's past and present failures. While white Americans memorialized their forefathers and made national icons out of men like Daniel Boone, black Americans constructed a version of the past that resembled aspects of the larger national narrative: fighting for national and individual liberty. While whites increasingly competed with one another along sectional lines to claim the Revolutionary past, African Americans—

voices nearly drowned out—spoke of a Revolutionary past that linked them together as a race that epitomized the fight for liberty, only to be denied the promise of the past. And yet that competing memory also validated the national construction of memory. Black memory—similar to black leaders' protest—functioned by mounting "challenges to racial inequality that appealed to cherished American values" but did not move beyond "the bounds of the American ideological landscape."[5] Like much of black protest, black memory challenged and affirmed the limits of change.

In 1851, William C. Nell, one of the first African American historians and a committed integrationist, published his preliminary account of black soldiers and sailors who fought for the United States in the American Revolution and the War of 1812. The previous year, the Fugitive Slave Act settled any qualms harbored by some free black Northerners and fugitive slaves about abandoning the country altogether, and thousands hurried on across the Northern border into Canada or left for Africa. A vocal free black minority had long advocated quitting the United States. The Fugitive Slave Act strengthened both their resolve and their case. Adding to their clamor, laws aimed at circumscribing the rights of free black men and women had proved a festering sore. Even laws successfully beaten back by black leaders and their few white allies served as a reminder that this relatively young nation had, from its inception, offered uncertain refuge for and unending attacks on African Americans. David Blight has noted that black intellectuals were reaching a crucial point regarding remaining faithful to their future in the United States. Nell's history answered these challenges. His answer sought to bind the nation to its black members and to bind African Americans to one another by creating a common memory. What that common memory included was important for building black identity. But it left out something equally important.[6]

Crafting black memory helped bind African Americans together by pointing to what nearly all their individual pasts had in common. Great diversity existed among the black population. It would be misleading to assume that black men and women all perceived themselves to be of one "race" with inherent similarities, and therefore common bonds and interests. White and black Americans were still in the process of figuring out exactly what "race" was. Race did not yet have the veneer of scientific precision that the late nineteenth century would use to delineate racial categories. Indeed, it was still a contested idea and not a firm scientific category. The evolution of notions of what race meant, or racial formation, progressed steadily among antebellum white Americans toward fixing African Americans into minstrel-like images of inferiority. At the same time, African Americans constructed their own concepts about race and tried to influence mainstream formulations of race. And though they refuted many of the assumptions and conclusions behind nineteenth-century racial conceptions, they did not refute one basic premise—that peoples of African descent, regardless of intermixture with European peoples, were of one "sable race."

Much of white racial formation, while drawing on particular physical similarities, was heavily predicated on notions of the other. White Americans tended to define themselves as a race by what they were not. They were not like other peoples whom they perceived to be outlandish, strange, barbaric, and decidedly not like themselves. Black racial formation similarly conceived of African Americans, slave and free, as one race based in part on certain physical similarities, but also drew heavily on memory of how black men and women endured and responded to past and present shared traumatic experiences of racial oppression. As free black writers and speakers shared memories, they engaged "in purposeful and explicit remembering as a form of empowerment and identity formation," a practice not uncommon for exploited minorities.[7]

By sharing memories, African Americans made individual traumatic experiences represent the whole, because virtually anyone who was black and living in the United States could identify with the kinds of stories told in slave narratives, described in black newspapers, or heard in church and in taverns. This even applied to second- and third-generation free blacks who had never been slaves. Marianne Hirsch, a literary scholar, has introduced the concept of "postmemory" in study of cultural memory of the Holocaust and defines it as the relationship of children to the experience of their parents who have survived "cultural or collective trauma." The children "remember" these experiences through the stories and images they grew up with—stories "so powerful, so monumental, as to constitute memories in their own right." Postmemory takes the past trauma of others and makes it part of one's own life history. In part, this is possible because of the "it could have been me" factor. Jewish children of Holocaust survivors knew it indeed could have been them. But it wasn't. Nonetheless, postmemory fosters an interconnectedness across generations; it recognizes the distance between the past and present while maintaining awareness of how little may separate subsequent generations from the experiences of their ancestors. For black Northerners in the nineteenth century, postmemory was even more complicated. Unlike the children of Holocaust survivors, the individual and collective trauma of slavery was not over; it was both a past and present event. The free descendants of slaves heard stories of people kidnapped from the North and taken into slavery. The "it could have been me" factor remained a cruel reality. For escaped and manumitted slaves, it had indeed "been me." The ongoing trauma combined with postmemory to create a process of forming ideas about what race meant that differed sharply in many respects from how white Americans formed their notions of race.[8]

Some similarities in the ideas about race did exist. But African Americans mixed in their distinctive memories of trauma. For instance, the *Colored American* brought race and heritage together when it ran an article that noted the distinct physical differences between the "5 general classes" of humanity, and then went on to describe physical characteristics that black people shared with all of humanity, such as the "same number of bones, muscles, nerves, and blood vessels." African Americans, then, like each of the five general classes, were distinct yet the same. But the article also linked African Americans with other Americans on an abstract level by noting nonphysical traits. On the question "that he possesses patriotism, let those white men who fought by him in the battles of the American Revolution, answer, Yes!" But unlike those white men, with whom he shared such fervent patriotism, liberty remained elusive for the black man. "After he bled and died to achieve it, [it] was denied him, even in this land of boasted freedom." Though sharing some of the same experiences as white Americans, black Americans used the past to help define what bound them to one another while separating them from whites. In the nonphysical, too, African Americans were the same, yet distinct.[9]

Present experience also factored into building black memory. Black Northerners incorporated recent experience such as the 1851 Christiana, Pennsylvania, riot into oral traditions, sermons, and print, providing a continual rebirth of memory and postmemory that reinforced black identity. When news spread about the Christiana riot, many African Americans interpreted black participants as heroes who fought in the tradition of their Revolutionary-era ancestors for American freedom. The riot began when four black men ran away from Edmund Gorsuch, their owner in Maryland. Gorsuch pursued, and a local group of black resisters in Christiana responded with deadly force—killing him. *Frederick Douglass' Paper* helped spread their translation into Revolutionary figures by printing news of a Columbus, Ohio, African Methodist Episcopal (AME) Church, which unanimously adopted a statement ensconcing the black resisters within the Revolutionary tradition. The "Christiana Patriots ... believing in the Declaration of American Independence, that 'all men are created free,' and adopting the language of the immortal HENRY, 'Give me Liberty or give me Death' ... taking the example of the Fathers of '76 as their guide" acted as heroes. It concluded by comparing "our Pennsylvania brethren" to the "manly and heroic stand taken by our Revolutionary Fathers."[10]

Black Northerners wove current actions tightly together with past events, making memory a simultaneous creation of what had happened and what was happening. Through this process of continually linking the present and the past, African Americans decided what their history meant, and most decided that it meant they were a race of people that had earned a place in the United States with full citizenship rights. As Ira Berlin's essay in this volume notes, memory is active in the present.[11]

Building black memory did not differ significantly from how or why other groups have constructed memory. Recollection of particular events is shaped by how those events are subsequently reported in media, how they are remembered by others, or simply how events are situated in the political, cultural, and social contexts of the time in which memory is being constructed. The process is a sort of "textual mediation." The text is the "stock of stories" maintained by individuals, organizations such as churches or private clubs, or institutions such as media or government. The oral traditions mentioned above are one kind of text. How African Americans used various texts to build black memory was heavily influenced by the context of antebellum society. Psychological research into individual and collective memory has noted that memory takes a variety of information, shifts it around, and builds it into a "general scheme" and is not necessarily "a matter of accurate recall of the isolated bits themselves." Researchers have found that people "are often quite good at recalling the gist of what happened, a process that involves selectively using, and often distorting or deleting, pieces of information that do not contribute to the overall picture they are reconstructing." For nineteenth-century Americans, that picture typically portrayed an imagined past that helped build national allegiance. Americans participated in building what Benedict Anderson has called an "imagined community." In many respects, black Northerners' construction and use of memory was no different.[12]

A personal example may help illustrate these concepts. As a teenager in the mid 1970s, my family visited West Berlin, a city that had a similar vibrancy to other Western cities we had seen such as London, Paris, and Brussels. Traversing the Berlin wall through Checkpoint Charlie was unforgettable. We went from a fairly prosperous, active metropolis to a drab, rundown, seemingly oppressive urban world. The contrast, which I had not been expecting, was unbelievably stark—at least it was and remains so in my memory. Two other events during our trip sharpened the contrast in other ways. First, the East German guards who came aboard our bus to check out what we might be taking in confiscated my comic books—even Spiderman! Second, when we returned, we were missing two GIs. This held up the bus for a while, until the soldiers were found in a park. We interpreted and remembered the delay and search as signs of the East Germans' insecurity and suspiciousness and assumed they believed we had dropped off spies (though perhaps they were just concerned about two lost GIs). The experience of going to East Berlin, more than anything else, informed my perspective on how communism was lived out. The political context of the Cold War undoubtedly reinforced that perspective. Our face-to-face encounter with communism occurred in a decade that was unkind both domestically and abroad for U.S. military personnel and their families. As an army brat—the son of a veteran who served three tours in Vietnam—my personal context also laid a foundation for that trip to have such an impact. That context also made the event seem even more "seminal" as the years passed and reinforced the importance of a memory that had helped justify the sense of mission and camaraderie shared by many military families.

Like most analogies, comparisons only go so far. But many of the principles work for antebellum African Americans. Living in a far more pervasively oppressive environment that steadily increased in racial hostility, the social and political contexts for African Americans heightened the significance of particular events. Individual black experiences of fighting in the Revolutionary War and the War of 1812, for instance, became all the more remarkable in light of the corporate experience of continually battling against attempts to deny African Americans their place as citizens. Individuals translated their experiences through retelling, abetting their circulation within black communities. Individual experiences eventually became a part of black oral tradition and were claimed by African Americans across the country as part of their story. And yet the process of building collective black memory differed painfully from that of other Americans. African Americans did not have to distort, shift, or imagine bonds of common experience when it came to dealing with severe racial oppression. They all shared these experiences. Many white Americans had shared experiences as well. The gist of Daniel Boone's experiences of making a life for himself on the frontier was shared by thousands of other frontier settlers. Yet most white Americans had not experienced a lifestyle anything like Daniel Boone's. Nevertheless, Boone became an icon—while he was still living!—for building American identity by helping white Americans to remember their past as a time of rugged individualism and freedom. Boone became a part of white Americans' shared past, a part of their collective memory, even though his experience had only been shared by a minority. In a country of "distinctive sections as well as value systems with conflicting self-images of one another and of themselves," this was an important function of memory. In an era when many Americans, particularly elites, worried that Americans were losing their memory of their noble past, ensconcing Boone fed a national desire to "inscribe on the public mind" certain understandings of the past. But for black Americans, every time they heard or repeated a story about loss, about denial of opportunity, about white insults and ignorance, it was truly a shared experience for virtually every black man and woman. This was life in these United States, and African Americans knew their experiences were synonymous with those who had gone before as well as those who struggled through the present. It took little imagination.[13]

Furthermore, black experience with racial oppression tended to be highly emotional, such as being separated from family members or being subjected to verbal or physical racial attacks. Social psychologists who examine how individual memory gets disseminated throughout a community argue that "every emotional experience tends to be socially shared." The more emotional an event, the more likely people are to share events within their circle of family and friends, and to do so repeatedly for weeks and months after the event. The circle of intimates who hear the story, far from keeping it confidential, typically relate it to their family and friends, and again do so repeatedly for months afterward. The "net result of this double process is that the script of a private emotional episode is spread across the social group, feeding the collective mind with the new social knowledge about emotions," and, of course, with new awareness of the precipitating event.[14]

What begins with the individual ripples out. Eventually, "individual and collective memory come together in stories of individual lives. The process of constructing a life story is heavily mediated by social construction; for example, it usually occurs in a social setting that shapes the stories told." That social setting helps shape what the event and the emotions mean, and how they will be used. When, as a teenager, I told my story of crossing through the Berlin wall to friends, the story helped construct and reinforce their perspectives on the seemingly titanic battle between freedom (the United States) and communism (the Soviet Union), akin for us to the eternal battle between good and evil. We interpreted the story's significance within the context of living on an army post in West Germany during a time of terrorist attacks on U.S. service personnel while the Cold War still raged. The dramatic (to us) event of having a new Spiderman comic book taken away helped spread the story as friends told others, "Did you hear about how the commie guards at the wall took Hancock's Spiderman away?" Social knowledge of the event spread, and the meaning of this particular memory was shaped by the context.[15]

My story, of course, did nothing by itself to shape the Cold War. But imagine how a stock of thousands of stories influence identity.

Ultimately certain stories take precedence, frequently because of their connection to well-known events or people. Certain experiences also become master stories because they embody meanings central to the maintenance and evolution of identity, support future goals, and represent the sum total of many stories. When individual stories of events—particularly if those events are experienced by more than one person—resonate with hearers on many levels, those stories are likely to be retold more frequently and eventually become part of a collective memory representing a common past. William C. Nell's work epitomized this process.

Nell's *The Colored Patriots of the American Revolution* and its 1851 precursor, *Services of Colored Americans in the Wars of 1776 and 1812*, did not uncover new ground for many African Americans. These works simply specified and consolidated the loose ends of stories and knowledge that had been passed around as oral traditions in black communities and had begun to appear in print. Tradition informed Nell as much as his own research, and appeals such as that made by the *National Era* in 1847 provided motivation. The paper feared that knowledge preserved within black communities of black soldiers' contributions was being reduced to "some faint tradition" that at best "lingers among their descendants." Nell laboriously compiled these stories from oral and printed sources as well as gravestones and military records. If Nell received information through third parties or indirectly, he sought further validation when possible. When William Howard Day, a prominent black leader from Ohio, wrote that he had "an authenticated chart, belonging to a soldier-friend" that demonstrated Andrew Jackson's dependence upon black soldiers during the Battle of New Orleans, Nell obtained confirmation from a U.S. Army report. When he lacked such verification, he provided contextual information in order to heighten plausibility.[16]

The manner of collection suggests the communal nature of this body of knowledge. As word spread about his work, people eagerly supplied information about relatives, friends, or stories they had heard and passed along. David Lee Child wrote to Nell in 1855, conveying a story that he in turn had heard thirty years before from a black Louisiana man. This Louisianan told Child how an African-born man had suggested that a barrier of cotton bags be built up to help thwart the British assault on New Orleans at the end of the War of 1812. Child acknowledged this might be mythical, but noted that Andrew Jackson's prejudices would have made the chance of a black man receiving credit for a strategically successful innovation highly unlikely, thus explaining the absence of an official account. Nell proffered contextual information: a sixteenth-century account of a similar breastwork being constructed to repel Portuguese invaders, presumably by soldiers "composed of various races inhabiting the cotton-growing zone of Asia and Africa."[17]

Nell spanned space and time, connecting black American patriotism with African origins. But Nell need not have depended on Child for this story. He probably used Child as his source because of Child's respected status among African Americans and to heighten credibility for a white audience. Several years earlier, the *Colored American* printed a brief article by a writer identified as T. V. R. who, anticipating further conflict with Great Britain, questioned whether African Americans should once again offer their lives to protect their country. The writer drove the argument home by remembering the same story. "What was the reward bestowed on the colored man that suggested the plan of making a breastwork of cotton bales? It is believed he was MURDERED."[18] Black postmemory had probably kept this story alive for decades as oral tradition.

Knowledge of black participation in the nation's wars obviously thrived in black communities. Child's source was a black man, and, more telling, the *Colored American* referred to this story with minimal context. T. V. R. knew black readers were familiar with the story and so eschewed detail. He also infused the tradition with purpose by placing it in the context of the debt owed to

African Americans by the United States, a debt for which African Americans sought settlement in the form of just treatment in the present. T. V. R. noted that "the colored people have always been among the foremost to take up arms in defence of this country, and what is our REWARD? oppression!" The veracity of the New Orleans soldier's story is not the concern here. The manner in which African Americans made the event function as memory, and to what ends, is of greater significance.

The *Colored American* quickly replied. The editor castigated T. V. R. for expressing sentiments the paper believed antithetical to the feelings of most African Americans. To decline participation now would be betrayal not only of country, but of "the noble spirit of our fathers," who, though suffering under slavery and oppression, were the "first when the shrill war trump's sound was heard." Despite the disagreement, a common theme emerged. Their forefathers not only fought, but apparently leapt without hesitation at the opportunity. T. V. R.'s response argued that black men had advanced the interests of the country in the past and should do so no longer until "*all* these institutions are thrown open to us on *equal* terms."[19]

The final salvo of this exchange came the following week, when T. V. R. endeavored to show the pivotal role black soldiers played in establishing institutions such as suffrage that the country now denied them. T. V. R.'s comments confirmed the tradition African Americans kept alive for generations, while at the same time noting the inadequacy of relying on supposedly reliable written sources. Here, by identifying the fundamental flaw in Western scholarship that made black people disappear through either the inability or outright refusal to recognize the value of the African oral traditions, T. V. R. preceded modern scholarship by over a century:

> In giving account of the services of colored men in the American Revolution, we are compelled to a great extent, to depend upon traditional instead of written history. It seems to have been THEN, as NOW, the settled policy of the *white* man, to have permitted the *colored* man, to an equal participation with himself in the dangers to

which they are exposed in securing Republican Institutions; but when secured, he is content to enjoy them alone, hence the entire absence, (almost,) in American History, of any mention of the noble achievements of colored men.

He then applied oral counterhistory maintained among African Americans. "Tradition informs us," he wrote, about the vital contribution of black participants. The "official" record did not credit a black man with saving Jackson's hide—and perhaps the country— at New Orleans, but the black record placed this African-born soldier at the center.[20]

Tradition informed African Americans. Tradition informed them about who they had been in the past, and who they were in their present. And the tradition belonged to all African Americans. T. V. R.'s comments point to how traditions, keeping alive stories of the past, translated into collective memory. The experiences of a few black men came to represent the experiences of all black Americans and attempted to serve the present needs of all African Americans. Proving one's actual genealogical relationship to those who fought was immaterial. All African Americans could claim Crispus Attucks or the African-born soldier who saved Andrew Jackson's hide at New Orleans. Memory meant pride and protest, heritage and inheritance. Memory built pride, a crucial commodity in an era of minstrelsy and virtually no positive depictions of African Americans in the dominant culture. Memory acted as protest. Simply the attempt to build pride among a people referred to as "degraded," not only by whites but even by black writers, served as a form of protest against popular culture's negative depictions, against those who attempted to write African Americans out of their place as free citizens in the polity, and even against other free black people who advocated emigration. Memory functioned as heritage by creating a genealogy of struggle for a people seeking fulfillment of the promises for which their ancestors had fought. And finally, memory staked out an inheritance that grounded their claim for full citizenship rights and opportunity. Free black writers and speakers commonly described this inheritance as a "birthright," imbuing it with legal character and all the legal rights guaranteed to an inheritor. This collective memory—which grew from history, black perceptions of that history, and the traditions that kept the stories alive—helped African Americans define who they were and why they could demand a place in the American polity.

Services of Colored Americans crystallized those functions of memory for the first time in one source. The slender volume chronicled black men who "do not fight from necessity, nor from mercenary motives, but from principle." And the principle was inextricably linked to American liberty. Nell proudly recalled John Hancock's presentation of the silk flag to the Bucks of America, "as a tribute to their courage and devotion in the cause of American Liberty." The flag, displayed publicly in 1858, operated as a material "site of memory" passed down along with an oral tradition that filled out the banner's meaning with a heritage of character and sacrifice. In this, black memory matched aspects of the dominant society's memory of the Revolution, which in the fifty years after the Revolution had emphasized sacrifice and the national character sacrifice had built. Black memory was, in a sense, enabled by an odd conundrum of twin national narratives of white domination and freedom. Often, "a cultural tool such as an appropriate narrative [allows] people to bring an experience into understanding." The paired national narratives of whiteness and freedom hastened the construction of black memory. The national narrative of gaining freedom through sacrifice provided an "appropriate narrative," creating a natural opening for African Americans to make sense of their own past, plug it into the national story, and speak it to a wider audience. African Americans could speak of sacrifice in patriotic terms perhaps more poignantly than any group of Americans.[21]

Beginning with Crispus Attucks, Nell sculpted a black patriotic tradition. Massachusetts blacks had already begun to memorialize their Revolutionary-era forebears when they asked the state legislature to allocate $1,500 for the erection of a monument in memory of Attucks as "the first martyr in the Boston Massacre." The legislature argued that another boy had been killed before Attucks and therefore denied the petition. The legislature's refusal was another prompt for Nell to place Attucks as the central figure of the massacre, which, according to Judge Dawes's 1785 characterization, was one of "the master springs which gave the first motion to a vast machinery [of] a noble and comprehensive system of national independence." Just a few months before Nell's book was published, the generally racist *Boston Transcript* attempted to cast Attucks as a "firebrand of disorder and sedition ... who, if he had not fallen as a martyr, would richly have deserved hanging as an incendiary." Nell countered by rendering Attucks as a black man who led others into an epic moment that unfolded into a momentous history. Other Massachusetts blacks concurred. In 1858, at the Convention of Colored Citizens of Massachusetts, the business committee stated that the "first blow in the American Revolution was struck by a colored person—Crispus Attucks— who fell as the first martyr ... thus ushering in the day which history has selected as the dawn of the America Revolution."[22]

The more radical William Wells Brown and other black leaders also invoked patriotic imagery that connected their forefathers' military participation to the fight for American freedom. Speaking to black men from all over the Northeast and Canada at the New England Convention in 1859, Brown underscored their right to stay in the United States in the face of colonization efforts by reminding the delegates of their heritage. "Then let us remain here," he proclaimed, "and claim our rights upon the soil where our fathers fought side by side with the white man for freedom." Similarly, the convention's president reminded the delegates that "some colored men, conscious of their manhood ... stood side by side with their white fellow-countrymen in the battles that secured the freedom and rights of a common country, felt, demanded and exercised the prerogatives of American citizenship." Brown reinforced the image of black soldiers as patriots and his black contemporaries as inheritors of the first black patriots' mission by urging the delegates to "stay here, and vindicate our right to citizenship, and pledge ourselves to aid in completing the Revolution for human freedom, commenced by the patriots of 1776." Nor was this claim upon a Revolutionary heritage limited to black Northerners. Throughout the antebellum era, free black Virginians, and likely other free black Southerners, fashioned memory and identity based upon their past military service while also using it to make a claim upon the tenets of liberty that the Revolution represented.[23]

Black leaders wrestled with an inherent tension that stemmed from claiming the United States as their rightful country while simultaneously distancing themselves from much of what the country represented. This complicated black memory. The leader of the Christiana riot, a free black man named William Parker, experienced this acutely. After the Civil War he called those who resisted slave catchers "true patriots" and declared "we have no country." The word "patriot," used frequently by black writers and orators, referenced commitment to a set of ideals commonly expressed within the context of the American past—in particular the Revolution and the Declaration of Independence. Yet at the same time, Parker seemingly repudiated the country. But it was not a contradiction as much as a juxtaposition. Like many black Northerners, Parker believed African Americans were patriots with a right to claim the country as their own, but the country's government refused to recognize that, thereby betraying the patriotic ideals. By rights, the United States was Parker's country; by circumstances, he was denied that claim. Parker voiced this tension just before he unleashed deadly force at Christiana. When his landlord's wife asked him simply to flee to Canada and avoid using arms, Parker replied that "if the laws protected colored men as they did white men," he would comply and appeal to those laws. However, he said, "the laws for personal protection are not made for us, and we are not bound to obey them. . . . [Whites] have a country and may obey the laws. But we have no country."[24]

Despite Parker's sharp ambivalence, his role was retold as a heroic one in the tradition of the American Revolution. But the manner in which Parker and Christiana were remembered reflects the complexity of black memory. *Frederick Douglass' Paper* placed him in a pantheon of freedom fighters that extended beyond American shores, trumpeting Parker as a man who "deserves the admiration of a Hannibal, a Touissaint L'Ouverture, or a George Washington." Still, the primary context in which Parker was grounded remained a distinctly American one. "A nobler defence," stated the paper, "was never made in behalf of human liberty on the plains of Lexington, Concord, or Bunker Hill than was put forth by William Parker at Christiana." The paper used the Revolutionary context as pointed protest. Parker and Christiana matched or exceeded the other touchstones of American memory and lived up to the ideals of what some African Americans were, in the 1850s, calling a "hypocritical Republic."[25] For many black Northerners, patriotism meant fidelity to the founding ideals, and though they were consistently expressed within the context of the nation, patriotism did not necessarily mean fidelity to the nation itself.

What may appear to be a paradox—black memory's persistent expression of a patriotic past existing alongside stinging rebukes and at times even rejection of the United States in the present—can be reconciled. T. V. R., Nell, Douglass, and other black Northerners drew upon traditions frequently centered on the highly emotional events of the American Revolution and the War of 1812. They selected a particular past, and the memory they constructed helped to identify themselves as African American—simultaneously distinct and similar with other Americans. Their past—their remembered past—informed them that they were Americans by right and by action. Their present told them there was something very wrong with America. Herein lie some of the roots of the "two-ness,—an American, a Negro; two souls, two thoughts, two unreconciled strivings; two warring ideals in one dark body, whose dogged strength alone keeps it from being torn asunder."[26] But the collective memory black Northerners developed aided in reconciling the early stages of double consciousness by making protest an integral a part of what it meant to be African American. As a part of black identity, black memory informed African Americans that they had a Revolutionary heritage to live out, and when they did, they were the "true" Americans. Black collective memory placed responsibility upon African Americans to maintain their claim on the country by continuing to protest, and extend their rightful heritage into the future by living up to the inheritance they fought for. Nell called African Americans of his day the "Patriots of the Second Revolution." For black Northerners, deep anger against one's country and support of people like William Parker, who emigrated, did not necessarily erase or even minimize their commitment to seeking fulfillment of the Revolutionary tradition that had become a part of African American identity.[27]

Preserving the past and making it an active agent in the present helped form an African American identity. When free black leaders employed the language of a military heritage (fighting for freedom) and connected it with labor (their ancestors helped build this country) they were building a common memory among African-descended peoples in the United States. Every black man and woman, whether Southern or Northern born, could point to laboring slave ancestors; most could not point to a genealogy of military service or some other clear connection to the American Revolution. But, like white Americans, African Americans extended the Revolutionary heritage to every black woman and man. Even Douglass, addressing the Colored Convention in 1853, referred to the cause "for which (nearly eighty years ago) your fathers and our fathers bravely contended, and in which they gloriously triumphed."[28] Instead of succumbing to the romantic racialism of the era or

accepting that they and slaves were bound together by white formulations of race, African Americans built a different conception
of race. They were a "race" in part because of their skin and, more
importantly, because of common experience and heritage. Building
and shaping a common memory was a part of how African Americans sought to bind themselves together, a task made urgent because
of the challenges they faced, such as the potentially divisive effects
of colonization.

A useful silence helped shape collective memory and the purposes it served. Maintaining memory meant forgetting as well as
remembering. And forgetting was a necessary part of making a
Revolutionary heritage a part of every African American's past.
Some of the forgetting involved individual stories. Nell liked to
recall the legendary king of Boston's black community, Richard
Crafus, also known as King Dick. As a child, Nell, like most black
Bostonians of the 1820s, knew Crafus, who stood well over six
feet and reportedly weighed around three hundred pounds. His
brief biography in *Colored Patriots* exemplifies how black Northerners remembered individual experiences as representative of the
black experience. Crafus was captured and imprisoned by the
British, as were many white sailors, but the national memory
tended to forget the impressments and capture of men of color.[29]
Nell's retelling renders Crafus not as a quiet captive, but one who
clearly declared himself an American citizen. Given Crafus's as-
sertive personality, this was probably accurate. Crafus's assertive-
ness also landed him in other jails, ones not associated with any
patriotic cause. During the 1820s, when Nell would have known
him, Crafus appeared repeatedly in Boston's Police Court. He appeared in court six times as a defendant for assault charges in 1825
alone. This pattern did not fit the patriotic portrait that black
leaders desired and did not appear in the collective memory.
Perhaps it was just forgotten, even by Nell. Current research by
neurobiologists, brain physiologists, and psychologists "has demonstrated that when we remember something from the past, it

comes forth largely constructed on the basis of present needs. . . . Built into our remembering then, or so it is argued, is a strong component of forgetting." That individual ability to wipe out what did not meet present needs appears to have been replicated on the larger canvas of collective memory.[30]

The useful silence broadened beyond individuals like Crafus to envelop the tens of thousands of slaves who fled to the British during the Revolutionary War, a few of whom even fought on land and sea against the American rebels. The silence was in some respects appropriate and accurate. Many of those who fled to the British had left with the British, many to slavery in the Caribbean, and some to a hard but free life in Nova Scotia.[31] In recalling the deeds of the ancestors, Nell had little compulsion to include those who were less likely to be direct ancestors of antebellum African Americans. This stood in contrast, however, with how black Northerners tended to cast black Revolutionaries as the symbolic descendants of all African Americans. When it came to those black men who acted in support of the American Revolution, black writers and speakers had little concern for accurate genealogy—whether or not black readers and listeners were actually descended from black Revolutionaries was immaterial. If indeed Nell and others remembered the thousands of slaves who ran to the British—often to toil under conditions worse than their previous circumstances—the mere fact that these men and women were not literally their ancestors should not have stood in the way of claiming them as a part of the African American past. But, similar to how white loyalists tended to be minimized or erased from American memory, black "loyalists" were clearly not included in any symbolic representation of the black American past.[32] Even though they struggled for their freedom as well—sometimes to the point of taking up arms and risking their lives—their stories simply had no utility for antebellum African Americans' fight for a place in the American polity.

Furthermore, at the first signs of hostilities during the Revolution some black Northerners signaled that their concern was personal freedom, regardless of whether it meant serving for or against rebelling white colonists. In 1774, a group of black men petitioned General Thomas Gage in Massachusetts for weapons and told him that other black men would fight for the British if they were rewarded with freedom. Abigail Adams believed this petition meant a conspiracy was afoot in Boston.[33] Their motives were clearly not to fight with "fellow countrymen" or for American liberty.

Personal liberty concerned these black petitioners far more than any national liberty, and the disorder of war, combined with the steady flow of runaways sparked by Lord Dunmore's offer of freedom to slaves who joined the British, provided a window of opportunity. Patrick Rael has noted that antebellum black "spokespersons let it be known that blacks owed their primary loyalty to liberty rather than to the nation." While black leaders never placed the nation above the greater principle of black freedom, they were also careful to avoid—or they had forgotten—the historical reality of some black forefathers who showed absolutely no concern for the new country or even actively opposed it. Those ancestors had gone too far.[34]

The silence regarding the thousands of slaves who fled to the British and the few who fought against American patriots—perhaps even against black Revolutionaries—is all the more striking because Nell's state-by-state account in his 1851 publication skips over Virginia and Maryland, which likely had the largest numbers of slaves who ran to the British in return for their freedom. Some slaves were actively recruited by the British as laborers, some ran because they heard about the offers of freedom, and some "joined" the British because their owners were loyalists and forced their slaves to accompany them. Sylvia Frey estimates the British removed about five thousand of Georgia's fifteen thousand prewar slave population by the war's end (though not all of these went willingly), and that thirty thousand of the quarter million slaves in Virginia "defected" to the British in just one year. Even taking into account that some did not go of their own accord, research has made it unmistakably clear that most of these slaves just picked up and took off amid the instability of war—and most ran toward the British, far more than the estimated three thousand black men who picked up arms against the British.[35]

Nell's expanded 1855 edition of *Colored Patriots of the American Revolution* made two vague allusions to the stream of black men and women who set their faces toward British lines, almost breaking the silence about the militant rejection of country. Both allusions squeezed into a context of slaves' love of liberty and inherent morality meant they would "take their freedom without murdering their masters" if the British came. Nell never mentioned the possibility that taking their freedom meant aiding the British against Americans because that would have undermined his central theme epitomized in the title. Labeling black Revolutionaries as "colored patriots" did not simply define the ancestors as patriots of freedom, but aligned them with the twin causes of liberty in general and American liberty in particular. Nell's tome had specific intertwined purposes: validating black American citizenship and building black memory. Either Nell knew of slaves' "defections" to the British and ignored it; or he and other African Americans had allowed those black men and women to slip from memory, which would be equally telling. Both suggest a purposeful forgetfulness, a desire to erase anything that might damage their case for citizenship or cause division within the race.[36]

The useful silence grew deeper. Black leaders ignored the reality that most black men fought for whoever looked most likely to win or whoever was in closest proximity—in short, whoever seemed the best bet for freedom. For the vast majority of black fighters, that meant the British. As Benjamin Quarles put it, "They reserved allegiance for whoever made them the best and most concrete offer in terms of man's inalienable rights, which is only to say that the loyalty of black Americans centered on the fundamental credos upon which the new nation was founded." During the Revolution, considering whites did not yet have a well-formed sense of national American identity, blacks would have been even less disposed toward fidelity to the new nation. Black men and women did not cast their lot with the Americans because of a commitment to an American nation. But when antebellum black leaders fashioned black memory, they attributed black progress toward freedom during the Revolution—and even long before it— to a distinctly American heritage. When the New York preacher Dr. James W. C. Pennington spoke to a black convention in Ohio, he cast the New York slave conspiracy of 1741 as an example of black people "being the first Americans whose bosoms were fired by the spirit of American Independence." That spirit, according to Pennington, carried into the American Revolution. But as Sylvia Frey has deftly argued, many black men and women viewed the American Revolution as a war of resistance not against Britain on behalf of the United States. They resisted slavery on their own behalf, regardless of slave owners' loyalties.[37]

Revolutionary rhetoric undoubtedly did genuinely stir some to commit to the struggle for a new nation. But when Nell, eighty years later, described black men as "those who...had warm hearts and active hands in the 'times that tried men's souls,'" he situated black Revolutionaries within a distinctly American tradition by calling forth the image of the grand struggle against British tyranny for the sake of American liberty. But it was a tradition and identification that likely would have been foreign to many of those black soldiers who fought to realize a "concrete offer" of liberty, regardless of who offered it.

The black patriotism of the antebellum era was clearly qualitatively different from the patriotism of most antebellum white Americans. Inseparable from the creation of an African American patriotic tradition was the uncompromising critique of the national failure of the United States to honor its ideals. African Americans did not flag in their efforts to keep national exploitation and hypocrisy a public matter. They had "a critical sense of their country's history, their condition permitting no easy escape into a national folklore." This was the qualitative difference. For African Americans, the creation of patriotic heritage was neither easy nor an escape. It was a necessary construction—a resurrection, perhaps—in order to further ground their right to full citizenship. But it was a construction nonetheless.[38]

As the antebellum era came to a furious close and war broke out over the country, the past, present, and future surged together for African Americans. Free black Northerners had long argued that in the Revolution, and especially at New Orleans in the War of 1812, they had played an important role in the maintenance of a national liberty still denied to their enslaved brethren and still abridged for most free blacks. Their future, and the future of the millions who remained in bondage, rested on the success of the Union. And they argued stridently for the right to help determine African Americans' future by doing what they had done in the past—fighting for freedom through military service. In this argument, the antebellum construction of black patriotic memory reached its fruition and stood ready for active service in the future.

Frederick Douglass gave black patriotic memory perhaps its most eloquent and notable voice. Early in 1862, he pointed out that the Union had foolishly decided to fight "the rebels with only one hand, when we ought to be fighting them with both." Holding forth the past as the model for the present and future, Douglass chastised Union leadership for clinging to a policy that had been true "neither in the Revolution, nor in the last war." He challenged the Union government, asking if "Washington, in 1776, and Jackson, in 1814, could fight side by side with negroes," why could the Union's generals not do the same? A year later, Douglass asked virtually the same question. "We were with you on the banks of the Mobile, good enough to fight with you under Gen. Jackson. Why not let us fight by your side under Gen. Hooker?" The racially mixed audience responded with loud cheering. Douglass's invocation of their shared past no doubt had special resonance with the black listeners. Letters to his newspaper echoed the theme that because "Africans fought well in the Revolution" and in 1814, black men should be able to lend their iron hand, as Douglass called it, to win liberty now and forever.[39]

Not all black Northerners agreed at the war's outset that black men should attempt to join the Union army. But, as T. V. R. did, these arguments still used black memory to build a case. In the weeks after Fort Sumter, the Philadelphia-based *Christian Recorder* put it plainly in its front-page article, "The Star Spangled Banner and the Duty of Colored Americans to that Flag." Sweeping the past "eighty-six years ago, when the thunder of the Revolution first pealed in the heavens" and when "the stars and stripes first floated upon the breeze over the battle-field of New Orleans" into the present, the paper sounded the trumpet call of black patriotism. "Where were the men of color," the paper asked—and answered, declaring, "Right by their country's side." But the writer demarcated a line between then and now. Where once the country had welcomed their service and acknowledged their citizenship, the country did so no longer. Therefore, "to offer ourselves for military service *now*, is to *abandon self-respect*, and *invite insult.*" The columnist instead called on African Americans to pray for victory.[40]

Though initially divided on supporting or opposing black enlistment—and eventually enlistment's proponents carried the day—African Americans were fairly unified about what their past was and what it meant. They used the experiences of black soldiers in the past to represent the past of all black Americans. Black men and women of the Revolutionary era who cared not a whit about American patriotism and those who had even supported the British were quietly swept under the historical carpet.

William Wells Brown's 1867 account of black troops in the Civil War consummated black memory from the antebellum era. Brown begins by recounting black participation in the Revolutionary War and the War of 1812. Like Nell, he recounted Crispus Attucks's role in the "the first act in the great drama of the American

Revolution." Unlike Nell, Brown did not surround Attucks with patriotic language in order to imbue him or other black Revolutionaries with the same kind of nationalistic fervor or commitment to country that white Revolutionaries supposedly had. Such rhetoric is lacking throughout Brown's history of black participation in the Civil War. Nonetheless, even in this more pointed and less patriotic history, there are some similarities to Nell and other antebellum constructions of black memory. Brown perpetuated the useful silence regarding the thousands of slaves who fled to the British. Brown also made no speculation regarding the motives of men like Peter Salem, whom Brown noted played a key role at the battle of Bunker Hill. Though not explicitly cast as fighting for their country, they are decidedly not cast as fighting for their own interests. Brown did mention that "many slaves were offered to, and received by, the army, on the condition that they were to be emancipated." He did not mention this to point to the possibility that some slaves may have fought for whoever offered them freedom. Rather, he addressed this in order to highlight the "inconsistency of keeping in slavery any person who had taken up arms for the defense of our national liberty."[41]

Brown's failure to mention Revolutionary War contrabands who escaped to British lines is all the more striking considered in the context of subsequent chapters. These Revolutionary War rebels—slaves who rebelled against their owners and fled to the British—would have fit well within the tenor of the book. Denmark Vesey, Nat Turner, Madison Washington (leader of the mutiny on board the *Creole* in 1841), all heroic rebels and freedom fighters, set the stage for the final rebellion of black soldiers against slavery in the Civil War. Madison Washington—who had escaped slavery once before only to be reenslaved when trying to rescue his wife—even ended up taking his fellow mutineers to British territory, where they all gained freedom. The parallels were easy. It would have been a fine opening for Brown to place the Revolutionary contrabands in his pantheon of black rebels.[42]

Ultimately, the first large group of black rebels vanished from African Americans' collective memory because they did not serve any useful purpose—and in fact would have countered the purposes of antebellum black memory. This ultimate counterhistory was too radical and could not be made to represent a past for all black Americans.

Memory appears to operate in some similar ways for African Americans today as it did for black Northerners in the nineteenth century. Black Americans then and now blur "boundaries of the personal and public, the individual and collective" when speaking of their heritage. Roots have historically "meant something broader" for blacks than for whites. Personal family heritage is often inseparable from the larger black struggles and successes. African Americans have historically constructed what I have labeled an oral tradition of counterhistory and Roy Rosenzweig and David Thelen have called "counternarratives" because their collective stories have been "quietly elbowed aside" by the dominant narrative, as the *National Era* had noted in 1847. African Americans continued the practice of building and maintaining their own narratives when the dominant society attempted to erase the crucial role of black participation in the Civil War. Black Union veterans, for instance, figured prominently in public African American celebrations that preserved black memory until World War I eclipsed their story. In addition to public celebrations, "orally transmitted history—as well as particular trusted books, films, and museums compete with an 'official' version of the past that is often distrusted." Interviewing contemporaries, Rosenzweig and Thelen note that despite their "forceful critique of mainstream history, African Americans still placed their experiences within American history." The roots of African Americans' proclivity to embed themselves within the marrow of American history lie in the first construction of black memory, and continue to shape black identity.[43]

Building that black patriotic identity, an identity tied to the struggle for freedom that had come to characterize the nation's founding, anchored free people of color in the North to a distinct black identity. The unflagging and unsparing protest and critique that African Americans promulgated throughout the early republic era flowed from this identity.

4

Black and on the Border

EDWARD L. AYERS,
WILLIAM G. THOMAS III,
and ANNE SARAH RUBIN

THE CIVIL WAR is often understood in terms of stark opposites. It seems only natural to think of North and South, of Union
and Confederacy, of freedom and slavery. But the habit of thinking
in opposites often extends to other parts of the war where it serves
us less well: battlefield and homefront, soldier and civilian, male
and female, and black and white, as if these places, people, and
experiences were not swept up in the same all-consuming war.

In an attempt to bring together aspects of the war that are often
kept separate, this essay focuses on the region of the United States
that is often ignored when explaining the onset of the Civil War:
the border where the upper South met the lower North. This area—
a third of the nation—went into the war with uncertainty but then
gave itself over to the conflict, playing a crucial role start to finish
as battlefield and supplier of soldiers, materiel, and leaders. Specif-
ically, this essay looks at the border between Virginia and Pennsylvania, a region almost arbitrarily divided by the Mason-Dixon
Line. People in this area had much in common—from their ethnic

heritage to the crops they grew—but were divided profoundly by slavery. This division made all the difference.

We start our story in Franklin County, Pennsylvania, whose southern border rests on the Mason-Dixon Line. Nearly eighteen hundred people identified in the census as black or of mixed race lived there in 1860. Indeed, Franklin held the fifth-highest number of black residents of any county in Pennsylvania. Black families had several reasons for living in the county. Eight out of ten had been born in Franklin. Slavery was well established in Pennsylvania in the eighteenth century and had been especially strong in the southern part of the state, where farms differed little from those just across the Maryland border. Several hundred free blacks, moreover, had come from Maryland and Virginia in the decades since.

Most black families lived near one another in small communities and in large households. They gathered several generations under the same roof or nearby, seeking security in a threatening world. Many gathered in the southernmost parts of the county, with nearly four hundred in Mercersburg. The other largest group of African Americans in Franklin lived in the South Ward of Chambersburg. They were unwelcome just across Market Street in the next ward, where only a few people of color lived. Most black people in Franklin's largest town worked in the same jobs as other black people throughout the North—laborers, porters, waiters, shoeblacks, cooks, and servants—and had just as little to show for it.

When the Civil War came, the black population of Franklin had not been welcome to participate in the preparations. Like their counterparts across the North, African Americans in Franklin had been turned away from the recruiting tables until early 1863. At that time Massachusetts—tired of waiting for national action—acted on its own and received authorization from its governor to create black regiments officered by white abolitionists and re-cruited from across the North.

Then the Fifty-fourth Regiment of Massachusetts Volunteer Infantry formed in Boston. At its head stood Robert Gould Shaw, the young son of a leading antislavery family in Boston and a veteran of another Massachusetts unit. Leaders of the abolitionist movement, black and white, raised over a hundred thousand dollars and began a vigorous recruitment campaign across the North from Massachusetts to Ohio. Everyone involved was determined to show that African American men were eager to fight for the Union and abolition, eager to put their lives on the line against a foe that decreed that any black man captured fighting against the South would be hanged for instigating insurrection. "The paper proclamation must now be made iron, lead, and fire," Frederick Douglass declared.[1]

In March, Franklin's Democratic paper noted with relief that "in this neighborhood, there has, so far been no effort to procure negro recruits, that we have heard of, and it is currently said that such an effort, if made, will be useless. They will have to be drafted, if obtained at all." White men in Franklin County and throughout Pennsylvania, bribed with bounties, were already being drafted to fill the state and local quotas. Certainly black men would not be braver.[2] Only a week later the paper admitted that "a negro recruiting officer visited this place last week and of course was quite a 'lion' among the 'free Americans of African descent;' but, as far as we know, he did not obtain a single recruit," the *Valley Spirit* reported. Rather than joining in the fight, the paper laughed, "it is rumored that one of the 'sable brethren' retorted to the urgent appeals of the recruiting officer in favor of his cause: 'Nigger has nuffin to do with dis war. Two dogs fight over a bone—did you ever see de bone fight?' "[3]

The paper could not have been more wrong. Only four weeks later, in late April, the *Valley Spirit* ruefully noted that "some forty or fifty black recruits for the Massachusetts Regiments, left this [community] for Boston, on Monday morning last." The paper, clearly surprised, blustered that "we are only too glad to get rid of these worthless negroes." Always eager to find something wrong with anything black people did, the paper whined that "we scarcely like the idea of their being credited to Massachusetts, and thus filling up her quota under the last draft, while Pennsylvania was compelled to fill her quota, under that same draft, with free white male citizens."[4]

The black men of Franklin would not wait for Pennsylvania. They seized the first opportunity they found to join the fight. An African American abolitionist recruiter from the Fifty-fourth Massachusetts, perhaps based in Harrisburg or Philadelphia, decided that Franklin County offered a promising field in which to recruit free black men. The details of his decision have been lost. Maybe the large percentage of African Americans in southern Pennsylvania attracted his attention; or allies on the Underground Railroad passed on word of the active community there; or leading black abolitionist Martin Delaney, a Franklin native, led the campaign; or Frederick Douglass recalled his visit there three years earlier, where black men had helped John Brown. In any case, forty-five men living in Franklin County enlisted in the Fifty-fourth and another thirteen signed up in the Fifty-fifth, the regiment formed by the overflow from the first regiment. Another eleven men born in Franklin County whose residence was listed elsewhere also signed up with the Fifty-fourth. These numbers made Franklin County perhaps the greatest contributor to these early African American regiments, on a per capita basis, of any place in the United States. Overall, Pennsylvania produced more black soldiers than any other Northern state, including Massachusetts.[5]

Ten of Franklin's recruits came from Chambersburg, but ten came from Mercersburg, the small community in southern Franklin where a large portion of the free black population lived. The Burgess family contributed two brothers and a cousin; the Christy family, four brothers; the Demus family, three; the Krunkleton family, four; the Rideout family, two; and the Watson family, two. Almost all of these men were young, between eighteen and twenty-five. They owned almost nothing and they worked as laborers and farmers, by and large, though Joseph Burgess was a teacher, Thomas Burgess was a carpenter, and Joseph Christy was a wood cutter.[6]

About a third of Franklin's black recruits signed up on the same day—April 22, 1863, almost exactly two years after Fort Sumter. The recruiting officers offered them a fifty-dollar bounty, thirteen dollars a month in pay (the same as white soldiers received), and eight dollars a month for their families left behind. Others joined throughout May as the Fifty-fourth gathered in Massachusetts, about a hundred men a week arriving at the gray and muddy camp outside of Boston. After an especially rigorous physical examination to choose the most fit, the new recruits were immediately put to drill and training. Supporters saw to it that all equipment and food were first-rate. Visitors, male and female, came to view the novel sight of black soldiers drilling. Among the visitors were William Lloyd Garrison and Frederick Douglass, whose son joined as sergeant major.

From Mercersburg, four Christy brothers—Samuel, William, Joseph, and Jacob—joined up with David Demus. The young Christy men lived with their father, Jacob, a widower of fifty-four who owned a small farm worth $200, and their sister Mary Jane, a twenty-year-old domestic worker. Demus had grown up a quarter of a mile from the Christys. He worked as a farmhand and married Mary Jane Christy in 1860. All of the men, in their early twenties, worked as laborers and held no property. The census taker categorized the Christys as black and Demus as mulatto. All of them had learned the basics of writing and sent letters back to Mary Jane about their experiences as they headed to Boston for training.

Jacob wrote first that "i take my pen in hand to inform to you that I am well and all the rest of them are well we are very well pleas with soildieren." He knew that "we wont have it so easy when we leave Boston we spect to leave about the first of June and it may be sooner for what we know for the rigiment is nearly fill out." The Christys arrived first, but soon Demus and his brother George appeared and wrote, "we was all very glad to see them boys coming." David sent word back to Mary Jane that "we di-dant no when we would get any money but i dont think it will be very long." The young husband was eager to send his wife money from his first pay draw.[7]

The training was hard and punishment came quickly. "Two of the boys was made go and get there knacksack and they had to wear them to punish them for looking aroung wile thay was in ranks when we are in ranks we are not aloud to look around or spite or to raise our hand." The discipline was worth it, though, for "we also gut our arms this day they are springfield rifles wich we have they are aloud to kill a great disants." The Pennsylvania men "dont like the climent atoll for it is very cold out here now we heft to wear our over coats all day it that cold." They knew that when they finished their training and "we go down south it will be worm enough and wormer then we wish."[8]

David Demus shared some of the same opinions of Boston in early May. "It is very cold here it snow and rain on the day that we lander." But he proclaimed himself "very well satify" and "very well pleas." He was glad to see that "we got in the nix Camp that sam and them other boys is in that left mercersburg." Like all soldiers, Demus longed for letters from home. He asked Mary Jane to "rite as soon as you can and let me no how mother is and all the rest of the friends."[9] Samuel wrote his sister the next day to let her know that "we expect to move soon to north carlina" because "the rigment ar ful now and we gut ar unform and arms." Samuel planned to send a likeness "as soon as i can git it taken" and asked Mary Jane to "tel father that i will send sum monney home to pay Clark for my boots as soon as we git ar buntey that will be soon."[10]

At the end of May the troops gathered to hear the governor of Massachusetts address them in inspiring terms and then march before cheering crowds through Boston. They boarded steamships to head for the Sea Islands off the coasts of Georgia and the Carolinas. Whites had abandoned the islands, among the wealthiest plantation areas of the South. "We was on the sea seven days befor we gut to Camp," Samuel Christy wrote home, "and after we weas

thear one day we went out to put up ar tents." After filling their
canteens and loading their haversacks, "we was March to the river
and gut on the ship and went a but fifteen mils thear was thee guns
bots with went be for us and at last we Came to a little town."[11]
The little town was Darien, Georgia, up the river from the coast.
The Fifty-fourth walked into the wealthy and nearly deserted town
of about one hundred homes. At their officers' orders, they stripped
it bare. The men got out "of the ship and went in to it and took
every thing that was good," Samuel told Mary Jane. "We gut
sum sheep and sum cattl and hogs and chickens and meny others
things."[12] David Demus calculated that "the hole amont Was a
boat a milion of dollars."[13] Officers' tents were soon equipped
with rich furniture, carpets, and mirrors.

After taking what they wanted, Samuel noted matter-of-factly,
the soldiers "set the town on fier and burnt it down." A white officer, James Montgomery, told Colonel Robert Shaw, "with a sweet
smile," that he wanted to destroy Darien because "Southerners must be made to feel that this was a real war." The white South
was "to be swept away by the hand of God like the Jews of old."
Montgomery had been an associate of John Brown's in Kansas and
shared Brown's belief in vengeance. Montgomery argued that the
Confederacy did not recognize the legitimacy of the black troops
and so "we are outlawed, and therefore not bound by the rules
of regular warfare." Montgomery lit the blaze in Darien himself.
Driven by the wind, it soon destroyed everything but a church, a
few homes, and a lumberworks owned by a Northerner.[14]

Shaw admitted in a letter home that "in theory it may seem all
right to some; but when it comes to being made the instrument of
the Lord's vengeance, I myself don't like it." He protested the burning to his superiors, fearing that it would reflect badly on the black
soldiers under his command. He had no doubts about burning a
town occupied by Rebels but the "wanton destruction" of Darien
seemed "dirty business." As the weeks passed, however, he came to

admire Montgomery and adopt some of his ideas about conducting war.[15]

The men of the Fifty-fourth retired to camps on St. Simon's and St. Helena near Hilton Head. The camps were pleasant, cooled by the breezes off the Atlantic. The black soldiers continued to train and drill, awaiting orders for further movements. In the meantime, orders from Washington cut their pay cut from $13 a month to $10, below that of white soldiers in the Union army. They heard rumors that their rifles would be taken away and replaced with pikes. The political pressure against the black soldiers remained strong in the North. Many whites doubted the black men would fight when faced with enemy resistance.

While the Franklin County members of the Fifty-fourth Massachusetts were down off the Atlantic Coast, ironically, Franklin County was being invaded. Franklin lay in the valley that runs from Pennsylvania all the way through Virginia. Accordingly, it had long been seen as one of the most vulnerable places in the North. When Robert E. Lee decided to take the war North in the summer of 1863 after the Confederates' stunning victory at Chancellorsville, he went up through Franklin, shielded from the east by the mountains.

There could be no doubt in late June that the Confederate invasion was a brilliant maneuver in every way. "Providence has abundantly blessed our movement, few casualties of any kind— and our success wonderful—we shall get nearly a million dollars worth of horses, supplies of all kinds &c from this county," Jed Hotchkiss wrote with satisfaction. Who could have imagined that invading the rich and powerful North would have been this easy? "The people are very submissive and comply, meekly, with the demands made on them—I think we shall be able to do a good deal towards bringing about an honorable peace."[16]

The Confederates did not live up to Northern fears. The demolition of a railroad bridge and roundhouse "were the only acts of real destruction attempted," Hoke acknowledged. "True, many horses, cattle, and other things were taken, but all was within the rules of war."[17]

One great exception to the "rules of war" marked the Confederate behavior: "the carrying away of free negroes." The Confederates' actions toward black people proved to be even worse than the white residents of Franklin had anticipated. "One of the revolting features of this day was the scouring of the fields about the town and searching of houses in portions of the place for negroes," Jacob Hoke lamented. "These poor creatures—those of them who had not fled upon the approach of the foe—sought concealment in the growing wheat fields around town. Into these the cavalrymen rode in search of their prey, and many were caught—some after a desperate chase and being fired at." Philip Schaff, down in Mercersburg, saw the capture of black people he knew "to have been born and raised on free soil."[18]

Rachel Cormany anguished over the raids. The Confederates, on the second day of their occupation of Chambersburg, "were hunting up the contrabands & driving them off by droves. O! How it grated on our hearts to have to sit quietly & look at such brutal deeds—I saw no men among the contrabands—all women & children." Like Hoke and Schaff, Rachel Cormany could see that "some of the colored people who were raised here were taken along." She could do nothing, only watch "on the front step as they were driven by just like we would drive cattle. Some laughed & seemed not to care—but nearly all hung their heads. One woman was pleading wonderfully with her driver for her children—but all the sympathy she received from him was a rough 'March along' — at which she would quicken her pace again." Rachel could not imagine what the Rebel soldiers "want with those little babies— whole families were taken." She assumed that the black men "left thinking the women & children would not be disturbed. I cannot describe all the scenes."[19]

The white people of Franklin did not always stand by and watch the kidnapping by the Confederates. Jacob Hoke interceded for two of his kidnapped neighbors and down in Greencastle "a few determined men, armed with revolvers, captured a squad which had in charge a number of these poor frightened creatures, and released them from the unhappy fate which threatened them."[20] A prominent Reformed Church theologian, Benjamin S. Schneck, went directly to Confederate headquarters to testify on behalf of Esque Hall, a "well and favorably known colored man," as well as for two repairmen on the Cumberland Valley Railroad.[21]

Jemima Cree took things in hand as well. She heard that the Rebels had been "scouting around, gathering up our Darkies, and that they had Mag down on the court house pavement. I got my 'fixens' on, and started down," she wrote her husband. "There were about 25 women and children, with Mag and Fannie. I interceded for Mag, told them she was free born, etc. The man said he could do nothing, he was acting according to orders." Fannie was indeed "contraband," so Cree could have done nothing for her. In any case, the Confederates left before the Franklin woman could take her complaint higher up.

"They took up all they could find," Cree wrote with terror and disgust, "even little children, whom they had to carry on horseback before them. All who could get there fled to the woods, and many who were wise are hid in the houses of their employers." Despite such efforts by white patrons, the numbers and guns lay with the Confederates, who captured "about 250 people... into bondage," Chambersburg merchant William Heyser estimated.[22] Amos Stouffer sadly observed that Confederates "are scouring the country in every direction about Waynesboro, Greencastle, Mercersburg [and] Finkstown for horses and cattle and Negroes."[23]

Wagons left Chambersburg with thirty to forty black women and children, heading for Virginia under the control of a Confederate chaplain and four soldiers. A group of local whites—led by the owner of a local inn—stopped the wagons, disarmed the soldiers, took them prisoner, and set the women and children free. The Greencastle residents decided that they risked the destruction of their town if they did not release the soldiers and so they did. But the chaplain demanded $50,000 to pay for the loss of the people he claimed as his slaves. Though he lowered his demands by half, the townspeople still did not have that much money. After threatening to return and burn the town, the chaplain left. A local reporter met thirteen of the captured African Americans voluntarily returning to Greencastle after they had heard of the threatened burning. They were going to turn themselves over to prevent retaliation against their friends, but were delighted to hear that the man who claimed to own them had departed.[24] The Confederates occupied Franklin County for two more weeks, until the beginning of July 1863. Then, they turned their vast army to the east to meet the Union army at Gettysburg.

Meanwhile, the African American soldiers of Franklin were engaged in battles of their own. "I have saw more then i ever expected to see be for i left home," William Christy wrote to Mary Jane Demus, after the Battle of Fort Wagner in July 1863. The charge, as he called it, up to Fort Wagner was a hard one. "We lost agrate meny men," Christy reported and concluded that "the revls Was tow harde for us." He also told his sister that their brother Jacob was wounded in the battle, that several friends from Franklin County were killed, and that her husband, David Demus, was also wounded. The charge at Fort Wagner, though, was not the only thing on Christy's mind. He was especially worried about his family back home and whether the rumors he was hearing were true.

When Confederate troops moved into Franklin County in late June 1863 just before the Battle of Gettysburg, they captured black residents and sent them South into slavery. The word spread and eventually soldiers in the Fifty-fourth heard the stories. William Christy thought it confirmed what he had always maintained, that "the rebels wood comin and take all the Coulerd poples that they cod get and take them." David Demus wrote to his wife to ask how she had "got a long" during the raids. The rebel troops, he stated matter-of-factly, were something he saw "evrey Day mor or lest." Demus told her that he had "sean so meney rebbel" that he hardly took notice when they start shelling his encampment, that he held little regard for them even though the shells hit "all a bote us and tha kill a man now an then."[25]

The Franklin County soldiers in the Fifty-fourth Massachusetts wanted at these times to go home—to protect their families from marauding Confederates, to spend time with them, to see their wives and children, to talk with their friends, and to eat decent food. David Demus told his wife that the hard tack they were issued was so tough that even after soaking it in water for eight weeks and stomping on it, the dull white substance looked and felt no different. "All we want is to get home," Demus wrote. The fleas were so miserable in camp that he could hardly stand it. He predicted that once he was home and alive it would take "all the Peape that is thear to hold me" to make him leave again. When Mary Jane Demus wrote to say that she was working hard in the fields husking corn, David Demus worried that his wife was doing too much hard labor and would hurt herself. "I doant Want to hear of you in the field," he emphasized. He reassured her that he would be paid soon and said to use his name and his imminent return to Franklin, if necessary, to prevent her employer from hurting her. Demus, the Christy brothers, and other members of the family all wanted to send and receive photographs or "likenesses" and wrote often to request them. Demus was concerned that his head wound, suffered in the attack on Fort Wagner, had so swollen and disfigured his face that his wife might not recognize him. Later, he wrote to assure her that he was healthy and even fat, since he was detailed to work as the butcher because of his wounds. When he learned from a Franklin County friend that his wife was also getting fat, he wrote to cheer her on, "how glad I Was to hear that you are getting a long so Well and is so fat . . . he told me that you Was that big and fat that you had to Com in the hose side Ways or you Wod fill up the dore he sead that he never saw eney boddy get so fat in a sort time in his life like you have got."[26]

The soldiers predicted that they would be home "before a great while." The Demus and Christy families in the Fifty-fourth kept up closely with each other. Jacob Christy reported that they "like soldieren very well but we dont like the thing of duing without money so long." With the weather pleasant and the hard campaigning of the summer behind them, the soldiers on Thanksgiving wished to be home and to have "sum turkey and chicken." Christy looked ahead to that time when they might come home and remarked, "we can tell you of things that you never drem of for I have seen thing that I never drem of before."[27]

The Demus and Christy family members signed up in Franklin County with the Fifty-fourth and fought with it through the war. They saw their fellow black soldiers drill and organize with professionalism. They saw their fellow black soldiers lead the assault on Fort Wagner and fight with bravery and dignity. They lined up in formation and saw a fellow soldier blindfolded, carted to a field on a wagon, pulled out of the wagon, stripped of his coat and shirt, put into kneeling position, and shot for desertion. "It was a hard site to lok at," David Demus wrote afterward. And they saw the death of one of their own. "We heave bean in a fite," David Demus wrote to his wife about the Battle of Olustee in Florida, "but thank god all ar boys got out but William Christy." Demus said that he saw his brother-in-law on the battlefield, saw him as he was shot, and saw him fall. "We lost him in a good [cause]," Demus told her, "he was a brave boy hear feared nothing."[28]

At home in Franklin County the black soldiers were given little respect despite the bravery they had shown in battle and the sacrifices they made for the cause. The Republican newspaper had supported black enlistment but in doing so pointed out that blacks were just as effective at stopping Confederate bullets as whites. The paper reprinted a song widely circulated from a soldier in the New York Irish regiment:

> In battle's wild commotion.
> I shouldn't at all object
> If Sambo's body should stop a ball
> That was comin' for me direct,
> And the prod of a Southern bagnet,
> So liberal are we here,
> I'll resign and let Sambo take it
> On every day in the year!
> On every day in the year, boys,
> An' wid none of your nasty pride.
> All my right in a Southern bagnet prod
> Wid Sambo I'll divide.
> The men who object to Sambo
> Should take his place and fight:
> And it's better to have a naygur's hue
> Than a liber that's wake an' white;
> Though Sambo's black as the ace of spades,
> His finger a thrigger [sic] can pull,
> And his eye runs straight on the barrel sights
> From under his thatch of wool.
> So hear me all, boys, darlings,
> Don't think I'm tippin' you chaff,
> The right to be kilt I'll divide wid him,
> And give him the largest half![29]

After the bravery of the black soldiers at the Battle of Olustee, the Republican paper praised the regiment generally but gave credit to the white officers of the Fifty-fourth Massachusetts. After Colonel Robert Gould Shaw's death at Fort Wagner, a similarly young and inspired colonel originally from Philadelphia led the regiment. The newspaper characterized the unit's behavior as "uniformly admirable." The Democratic press, however, could find no reason to support black soldiers in the fight and, instead, lampooned the Fifty-fourth. The *Valley Spirit* reported the Battle of Olustee as a "disaster" and said it was "mainly due to the cowardice of the colored troops." The paper predicted that "before the war is over the negro will not be found as brave, enduring, or efficient as the white." For good measure, the editors scoffed that if the black soldier proved otherwise, then "all history [is] a fiction." The Fifty-fourth and the other units of the United States Colored Troops (U.S.C.T.), they maintained, were the "colored pets of the administration" and the government was systematically covering up their poor performance on the battlefield.[30]

There can be little doubt that the black soldiers in the Fifty-fourth heard these sentiments. Jacob Christy was not willing to let them go unchallenged. "We have been fighting as brave as ever [there] was any soldiers fought," he wrote his sister. "I know if every regiment that are out and have been out would have dun as well as we have the war would be over." Christy's war was becoming, if it had not always been, a war of rights and power, a war of demonstrated black claims to them. "I du really think," he wrote, "that its God['s] will that this ware Shall not end till the Colord people get thier rights." For white people who resisted what was happening and what was coming, Christy conceded that "it goes verry hard for the White people to think of it But by gods will and powr thay [colored people] will have thier rights." The coming of a new era of rights and power was on Christy's mind, and he admitted that some of those "that are liveing know may not live to see it." The sacrifices were worth so much to Christy because they would be made in the service of future generations. Christy made clear his commitment. "I shall die a trying for our rights so that other that are born hereafter may live and enjoy a happy life."[31]

A month later Christy's and Demus's hopeful sense of purpose and self-sacrifice turned partly to frustration. They had not been paid in months and both wrote home about the intolerable situation. Demus reported that the army might try to discharge both the

Fifty-fourth and Fifty-fifth Massachusetts, send them home, and then offer the men reenlistment at half the monthly wages (from $13 per month to $7 per month). He thought that even with less pay, "a bout the one halfe will inlis a gan." Christy complained that even though "all colard troops fights well ... thay are getting nothing for it." The abuse was almost too much to take, especially since the black regiments had been put into battle to make near impossible charges, and Christy suggested that the black troops might refuse to "run ourselfs in to placers were we well be slaughter up." With a tone of bitterness, Christy noted that the black troops had "dun enough of it to know how it gose."[32]

While Christy and Demus and the soldiers in the Fifty-fourth Massachusetts waited on Morris Island at Hilton Head in the summer of 1864, Confederate cavalry moved into Franklin County in retaliation for the Federal campaigns in the Shenandoah Valley earlier in the summer. Under the command of General Jubal A. Early, the Confederate forces demanded levies from Frederick, Maryland, and Chambersburg, Pennsylvania, after they threatened Washington, D.C., in late July. When they did not receive the money, the Confederates burned the town of Chambersburg and raided the surrounding countryside. Confederate clerk and former newspaper editor Joseph Waddell in Staunton, Virginia, thought the reprisal burnings were sure to further enrage the Northern people and revive their "war spirit." "The Yankees," Waddell predicted, "will come back and burn a hundred for one." Waddell considered the Confederate raid bad policy because the Confederacy's only hope was that Northern public opinion would demand an end to the war. The raid, he thought, would only enflame public opinion. He also thought that "it would be far better to let their outrages stand out before the world—... to the disgust of even some of their own people."[33] Waddell's opinion on this matter hardened and he later called it "a miserable affair, ... horribly stupid ... a blunder." Though after the burning of Chambersburg, Waddell admitted feeling a certain degree of pleasure that "the miserable Yankee nation, who have been burning and pillaging throughout our own country for so long, have now been made to suffer in their own homes."[34]

The black soldiers in the Fifty-fourth Massachusetts heard about the raid and wrote home to make their feelings known. David Demus was pleased to find out that his family "got of safe," and he wanted to convey how little he feared Confederate forces. "I am sorry that I ant thir," he wrote to his wife, "fer i heave saw so meney that a rebbel is no mor then one of ar one men." His brother-in-law was more direct and could hardly believe that the town men, white men, "let two hundred rebels come and burn the place." It was sheer cowardice, he seemed to suggest. "For i am a soldier," he explained, "and I know what fighting is." Christy stated with confidence that his company of eighty soldiers "can Wipe the best 200 rebels that thay can fetch to us." And another of Christy's brothers in the Fifty-fourth wrote home that he was "not a fird of all the rebels that Ar in the South."[35]

After the Chambersburg burning, Federal troops moved through the upper Shenandoah Valley in the fall of 1864 to try to crush Early's forces there. As they moved south into the valley, the Federal troops did not just burn Confederates' barns and liberate Unionists from prisons—they freed many black people in slavery. While slaves were running away throughout the war, the pace picked up in 1864 in the Shenandoah Valley. Civilians took notice. The newspapers were reluctant to admit the hemorrhaging loss of black labor and the visible recruitment across the South of black troops into the Federal army. The most the *Staunton Vindicator* would allow was a veiled comment that "only white labor is available locally."[36]

Confederate civilians also took notice when the Union army began to use black troops in Virginia. Amanda Edmonds, a young white woman at home on a plantation in the valley, chastised General Ulysses S. Grant for bringing "the abominable wretches and negroes to the field." Later in the summer when black soldiers in the Ninth Corps led a forsaken charge into the crater at Petersburg and were slaughtered, some civilians in the valley expressed paternalistic pity. Mary Cochran thought the black soldiers were "poor wretches stimulated with whisky and induced to think they would meet with no resistance." She considered it laughably predictable of the Federal officers and a sad betrayal of simple black men, whose white masters presumably knew much better what they were good for.[37]

When the Federal army came into an area, though, many African Americans took the opportunity to leave with it. In the Shenandoah Valley, Eva Honey Allen, a young white woman living near Fincastle, heard many rumors about the Federal troops. "Their doings are 'as thick as blackberries,'" Allen recorded. She was most troubled by the rumors that "the Negroes" on her plantation were relating, and called these "very alarming." One rumor spread that Hunter was coming with "a very large army, including 8,000 Negroes." Another story circulated that two or three hundred Negro men came from the Bedford area and joined the Federal army to make war on the Confederates. Still another report she heard from slaves ran that the Federal army "can't take the women off now, but will come back for them."[38] The Federal army impressed both free and enslaved African Americans in the Valley. In Staunton, Confederate clerk Joseph Waddell witnessed "a considerable number of Negroes" went off with the Federal army. The Federal officers apparently promised to take any African Americans willing to go with them to Washington, D.C., where "they could work for a living." Waddell, like Cochran, sneered at such a possibility and considered blacks too deluded or infantile to know what was good for them. Confederate civilians simply could not admit to themselves that slaves were disloyal to the Confederate cause or to their masters or that black soldiers might fight for rights and family and freedom.[39]

Black soldiers saw with their eyes events that Confederate civilians and some of their fellow Northerners could not comprehend. John M. Christey fought in the Petersburg campaign at

Chaffin's Bluff. He thought the bullets whistling in the air might kill him during the battle, but instead he survived and helped his U.S.C.T. unit drive the Confederates back and "cut them all to peces." The troops buried five or six wagonloads of dead Confederates that day, and Christey said that every day Confederates were deserting "as fast as tha can . . . by the hundreds . . . day and night." The Federal officers praised the U.S.C.T. units, and Christey was proud to report that "We fote the Best of eny new regment that ever tha sen com on the fild to fite tha could hardley get them to stop firing at the Johneys."[40] When Federal black troops were first deployed in Virginia in June, Confederate women expressed outrage in their diaries. One woman wondered whether the Confederates would "ever blot out such a foe," one that seemed to stop at nothing to win, one that used black troops to fight the war. Later in September after the black troops had won several engagements around Petersburg, her question changed. "Will kind Providence forsake us in this day of adversity? Will he permit one of the most beautiful countries in the world to become enslaved and subjugated?"[41]

The last months of the war impressed upon Confederates that the war itself and their perceptions of the war were in constant negotiation. The pastoral farms of many planters and yeoman were wrecked, barns burned, cattle driven off, and crops seized. Lee's army conscripted nearly every available man, while it lost battles, cohesion, and moral direction. Eva Allen's brother, Henry, who was on duty in the trenches at Petersburg, wrote home to tell of a strange story of a "Negro man belonging to old Capt. Breckinridge." The former slave fled the plantation and "went off with Hunter" in June 1864. According to Allen's brother, Henry, the man deserted from the Federal army and came over to the Confederate lines. He told them "he was 'sick of soldiering,' and said there were some other Botetourt Negroes in his Regt. all anxious to get back home." Henry was amazed at the strangeness of the report, not because a former slave in the Federal army had deserted to the Confederate lines, but because slaves were actually fighting in the Federal army. "Who would have thought four years ago," he wondered, "that the time would come when we would be fighting our neighbor's Negroes?"[42]

While Henry Allen expressed surprise at the presence of black Union troops, many of his fellow Confederates expressed deep animosity. The *Staunton Spectator* described the reaction in Winchester when a black regiment occupied the town during the spring of 1864. Seized by "indignation and disgust," some thirty local boys reportedly flocked to Confederate ranks, an occurrence that, the *Spectator* noted approvingly, "is more or less the case throughout the border wherever these black regiments have made their appearance."[43]

Virginians and other Confederates were just as aware of the symbolism inherent in black enlistments as the soldiers themselves were. David Demus of the Fifty-fourth Massachusetts believed that if it had not been for the black troops, the war would last another ten years. He also thought it "plane to see" that if the black soldiers had not fought, then black people would not be in a position to claim full citizenship. He considered "us Colard Men" the cause of "this ofel [awful] Rebelon."[44] From the Confederate perspective, any attempt to grant manhood to blacks was a threat to the Confederacy. Or, as the *Charleston Mercury* had argued when it was confronted by the men of the Fifty-fourth Massachusetts in 1863, "our slaves are to be made our equals in our own country, fighting against us."[45] That was, of course, an unacceptable challenge to Confederate identity and honor.

But what would happen if slaves were to fight for the Confederates? Just as white Southerners understood the implications that enlistment had for black manhood and citizenship, so too did they recognize the manpower advantage that black troops conferred on the Union. As early as 1863, influenced by the presence of African Americans in the Union ranks, some Confederates had discussed the idea of formally arming and enlisting slaves. The sticking point was always emancipation. How could slaves be asked to fight for Confederate freedom, without being granted it themselves? And to emancipate slaves, for any reason, was to call into question one of the very foundations of Confederate identity. But as the Confederacy faced mounting losses of territory and an associated plunge in morale during the winter of 1864 to 1865, debate over the proposal began in earnest. Backed by both Jefferson Davis and the Confederate cabinet and Robert E. Lee, the proposal to arm slaves forced Confederates to confront the question of what, exactly, they were fighting for.[46]

On November 7, 1864, Jefferson Davis sent a message to the Confederate Congress in which he called for the employment of slaves in a variety of noncombatant positions, while leaving open the possibility that "should the alternative ever be presented of subjugation or of the employment of the slave as a soldier, there seems no reason to doubt what should then be our decision." In so doing, Davis made explicit the great contradiction of slavery, since he acknowledged that slaves were not just property but people as well. As such, they could not be expected to work hard for a cause that would result in their permanent enslavement, and thus Davis also suggested that any slave employed in the army should be made eligible for a form of gradual, compensated emancipation.[47]

Predictably, Davis's suggestion was met with scornful, even angry, opposition. By suggesting that at some point in the future the Confederacy should think about turning to slave soldiers, Davis had brought to the surface simmering questions about the meaning of the Confederacy. Could a nation born out of the desire to defend slavery at any cost survive emancipation, even emancipation on its own terms? Davis and the other supporters of arming slaves argued that in fact they were protecting the "peculiar institution." Emancipate a few slaves in order to win the war, they claimed, and preserve slavery intact for others. Let the Confederacy be destroyed, and slavery would be lost forever. As an added benefit, support for any level of emancipation demonstrated to foreign nations and wavering yeomen that this was not a war exclusively to preserve the property of a wealthy few. Indeed, rumors still flew that this demonstration of Confederate determination to avoid "subjugation" would be just the thing to inspire British or French intervention.[48]

Essentially, supporters of arming slaves were making a pragmatic argument. The Confederacy was dying of a manpower shortage, and slaves could fill it. For many Southerners, the meaning of their new nation had changed. Protection of slavery was no longer their paramount concern. But, to other Confederates, particularly those in the Deep South, such a suggestion was anathema, tantamount to an admission of defeat. The *Staunton Republican Vindicator* reported that the *Savannah (Ga.) News* refused to publish any letters about the possibility of placing slaves in the army, on the grounds that such a question was not proper for a "newspaper discussion." The *Charleston Mercury* warned ominously that "the freemen of the country are not dependent on slaves," and should they not work out their own "redemption," they would become "the slaves of their slaves."[49]

Charleston's defiance seemed reckless closer to the border. Virginians felt their region had borne the brunt of war and were perhaps more willing to think creatively about strategies for achieving peace. Peace, however, had specific meanings—independence, not surrender—and the measures to win freedom might not be the same as those that would preserve slavery. In Staunton, Joseph Waddell confided in his diary that "I greatly prefer independence without slavery, to submission with it, and would be glad enough to get rid of it if I could see any way of disposing of the negroes without giving them up to barbarism or annihilation."[50] By February, with the Confederacy's military fortunes looking even more bleak, Waddell seemed less sanguine. Now he saw talk of enlisting slaves for what it was—"a concession of despair," rather than the "virtue of necessity" that Robert E. Lee would have had Confederates believe. For Waddell, however, the most problematic issue was not the abolition of slavery per se, but the upheaval that would surely accompany emancipation. Already, he noted, Augusta's slaves had heard of the enlistment plan and were "greatly troubled," and he "shudder[ed] at the prospect" of wartime emancipation.[51]

Waddell's grim forecasts ran counter to another trend in Confederate opinion in early 1865. Following the failure of the peace mission in early February, and the attendant realization that there was no chance for a negotiated end to the war, the Confederacy actually enjoyed one last burst of martial spirit, one last gasp of the old bravado that had characterized the early years of the war. The *Richmond Enquirer* boldly declared that the enlistment of slaves would not only strengthen the armies "without doing the least injury to the institution of slavery," but would also increase discipline amongst white troops. The soldiers of the Fifty-sixth Virginia unanimously declared that "if the public exigencies required that any number of our male slaves be enlisted in the military service in order to the [sic] successful resistance to our enemies and the maintenance of the integrity of our government we are willing to make those concessions to their false and unenlightened notions of the blessings of liberty, and to offer to those, and those only who fight in our cause, perpetual freedom as a boon for fidelity of service and loyalty to the South." These Virginians subscribed to one of slavery's perennial misconceptions—that slaves did not know what was best for them, that they did not all want to be free. Somehow, Confederates wanted to believe that they still controlled the survival of slavery, that they could free some slaves to fight to keep others in bondage. In this, they demonstrated a willful ignorance of their slaves' inner lives.[52]

The debate over enlisting and arming slaves went back and forth during the fall and winter of 1864 to 1865. Robert E. Lee had long supported the plan, but privately. He finally entered the public discourse over this issue in mid-February 1865 with a letter that shifted public, and congressional, opinion squarely to the side of enlistments. In his letter to Congressman Barksadale, reprinted in newspapers throughout the Confederacy, Lee explained that the measure was "not only expedient but necessary." He went on to answer another criticism, one familiar to Northern black soldiers as well—the question of whether blacks would make good soldiers. Lee felt that they would, explaining, "I think we could do at least as well with them as the enemy, and he attaches great importance to their assistance." Lee cited the slaves' physical strength and "habits of obedience" as reason to believe that they would serve well, especially if induced to service through the promise of freedom. He went even further, suggesting that a draft of slaves would be unnecessary and counterproductive, preferring instead to call for slave volunteers, a measure more likely to "bring out the best class."[53]

By this point, Lee and his ever-shrinking Army of Northern Virginia had become the focus of Confederate hopes, and his opinion bore more weight with the general public than anyone else's. His letter was reprinted with approving comments, and inspired more serious, more public discussion of the future of Confederate slavery. Citizens of Augusta County, Virginia, held a mass meeting in late February at which they condemned "the course of the United States in proposing to tear away the last vestige of our rights as a condition of peace," and expressed their support of arming slaves. They expressed their deep faith in Lee, concluding simply that "we shall not stop to discuss abstract questions, but will cheerfully give our servants, as we have our sons, to our country." What was left unspoken, though one can hardly believe unthought, was that the lives of their slaves were not the Virginians to give.[54]

Confederates' last ditch effort to save their nation by weakening slavery came too late. Their slaves had taken matters into their own hands, and the Union army was helping them. As the war came to a close in April 1865, the black troops were still in the field fighting Confederates, liberating slaves, and turning the war on the civilians. Marching out from Georgetown, South Carolina, in early April, Joseph Christy's Fifty-fourth Mass. went into the field "to hunt the Johneys." Christy reported, "We found them too and kild a grate meney of them." They fought for six days, and according to Christy, the Fifty-fourth burned down houses, captured and burned railroads, and freed over a thousand slaves before they heard that peace was declared. Christy called the long line of freed peoples following the Fifty-fourth on the road back into Georgetown "one of the grates sits that i ever seen."[55]

After the war was over, the men were slowly discharged and the Fifty-fourth Massachusetts disbanded. For the soldiers who had fought for over two years to define their freedom, to liberate others, and to defeat the Confederacy, the summer of 1865 was a time of reaping the harvest. Jacob Christy did not want his discharge until the Fifty-fourth was officially and completely disbanded. He wanted to stay with "the old Regiment As long as she is together." He wanted to be with it to the end, to demonstrate for the whole world what it meant and had accomplished. "I come away from Massachuettes with it," he declared, "and I want to go back with it to march through the city of Massachuettes agian." He wanted the people of Massachusetts to see the ripped, fraying, and bullet-riddled battle flag and to see with their own eyes what the regiment had done. "Just to look at it," he thought, "any body can tell what we have been dueing we fought hard a many A time for them."[56]

As for the former Confederates in the summer of 1865, black soldiers gave them little room and extended no reconciliatory gestures. Not that Confederates would have been willing to accept them. On the streets of Charleston the men of the Fifty-fourth Massachusetts asserted themselves in ways the former Confederates could hardly believe. "It goese verry hard with them," Jacob Christy said of the former Confederates. The black soldiers expected them to give way on the streets not the other way around, and when they did not, Christy reported, "we knock them out of our way And if thay dont like that we take them up and put them in the Guard house." Christy and the men of the Fifty-fourth went further on some occasions to demonstrate how much the war had changed. They went into the streets of Charleston "just to get them [former Confederates] to say something out of the way so that we can get at them and beat them."[57]

5

A Stranger in the Club: The Army of the Potomac's Black Division

NOAH ANDRE TRUDEAU

THE DECISION to add African American units to the Union army was a massive experiment on virtually every social, military, and personal level. The experiences of the soldiers themselves were complex and varied. There are many ways to tell their stories. This one follows the brief history of the only black division organized in the Civil War to be made a part of what is arguably the best-known Union force of the period: the Army of the Potomac. Termed by a postwar historian the "mighty rival" of the South's equally illustrous Army of Northern Virginia, the Army of the Potomac had a history, tradition, and command rank culture that set it apart from other Northern armies. This brief examination of its reluctant involvement in integration hopes to illuminate a lesser-known chapter of America's most studied war.

This tale begins on January 7, 1864, when Major General Ambrose E. Burnside began reconstituting the Ninth Corps (widely dispersed on outpost duties) for active service in the east. In a memoranda sent to Secretary of War Edwin M. Stanton on January 26, Burnside asked that "permission be granted me to organize a division from the colored troops ... comprised of infantry, artillery, and cavalry." Responding three days later, Stanton said, "No objection occurs to me in regard to the organization of a division of colored troops." Burnside's biographer, William Marvel, suggests that this eagerness for black soldiers on the part of an otherwise socially conservative officer was as much a reflection of his need for manpower as it was an evolution in his thinking.[1]

Regiments, white and black, soon converged on Annapolis, Maryland. The black division that took shape under Brigadier General Edward Ferrero initially consisted of five full regiments (three organized in Maryland, one from Ohio, and one from Pennsylvania) and a partial regiment from Connecticut. While the motivations for enlistment were no less varied for black individuals than they were for white, the words of one Pennsylvania African American recruit speaks to a core purpose. "I hope that the day is not far distant when we shall see the colored man enjoying the same rights and privileges as those of the white man of this country." Another Pennsylvanian in the ranks, Sergeant John C. Brock, recalled the march from Baltimore to Annapolis for Philadelphia's *Christian Recorder*. "We found the road, as we went out, lined with tents and soldiers, all of which cheered us as we passed.... God speed the glorious work, and may this accursed rebellion, that has been producing so much sorrow and distress, be brought to its proper doom." The reception given the Ohio regiment was far less celebratory. According to a white officer in its ranks, the men were stoned by "low people" near Pittsburgh.[2]

By the end of April, when the Ninth Corps was ordered to join the Army of the Potomac near Brandy Station, Virginia, it was decided that the men would parade through Washington en route. On April 26, the corps formed up on the capital's outskirts and marched south down Fourteenth Street past Willard's Hotel. Waiting on a second-floor balcony to review the troops was a small crowd of notables, including the sideburned Burnside and President Abraham Lincoln.

The last to march by Willard's were the black troops, the first that Lincoln had ever formally reviewed. Charles Coffin, a reporter for the *Boston Journal*, described the moment as one of "sublime spectacle." "Accoutered, as we were, with a full complement of clothing, etc., and the day being very warm, the march from outside the city until across Long Bridge, without a stop and with cadenced step, was very trying," recalled Captain James H. Rickard of the Nineteenth United States Colored Troops (U.S.C.T.), "but not a man left the ranks until the bridge was passed." As Coffin observed, the president acknowledged the African American soldiers with "dignified kindness and courtesy." But the discipline of only a few weeks was not enough to hold the former slaves in line as they recognized the man who had issued the Emancipation Proclamation. "They swing their caps, clap their hands and shout their joy," Coffin reported. "Long, loud and jubilant are the rejoicings of these redeemed sons of Africa."[3]

For the moment, military protocol kept the Ninth Corps separate from the Army of the Potomac; Ambrose Burnside ranked Major General George G. Meade who commanded the army. Grant's solution was to have Burnside report to him for orders, but for all other purposes the Ninth Corps was a part of the military force that, on the night of May 3, began what is known as the Overland Campaign. The black division was enlarged by a Virginia regiment and split into two brigades: the First, led by Colonel Joshua K. Sigfried, and the Second by Colonel Henry G. Thomas.

On May 5, when the Army of the Potomac began a series of engagements against General Robert E. Lee's Army of Northern Virginia that would extend into early June, Burnside's black troops were assigned a supporting role. When they moved up from guarding wagons into a reserve position on May 7, they were seen for the first time by many of the Army of the Potomac's headquarters staff, one of whom was a Boston patrician named Theodore Lyman. "As

I looked at them," Lyman observed in a letter to his abolitionist friends, "my soul was troubled and I would gladly have seen them marched back to Washington.... We do not dare trust them in the line of battle. Ah, you may make speeches at home, but here, where it is life or death, we dare not risk it."[4]

Once the campaign became a series of flank movements by the Union army, the job of protecting the rear was given to Ferrero, whose two black brigades were augmented with three white cavalry regiments for the task. This assignment led them to minor combat actions on May 15, near the Alrich farm, southeast of Chancellorsville, and on May 19, a few miles west of Salem Church, outside Fredericksburg. Word quickly spread along the army grapevine that the black troops had stood to the job. "Their conduct was above criticism," was how one Pennsylvania soldier put it.[5]

In these first marches and movements some of the black troops fell into enemy hands. This was the first time that armed African American soldiers were taken prisoner in this theater of operations, but their fate differed little from that being suffered by their western comrades. Charles Hopkins, a white soldier who had been captured during the Wilderness fighting, was witness to the hanging of a black POW at Orange Court House on the morning of May 9. An even more chilling incident is related in a matter-of-fact entry for May 8 in the diary of a Virginia cavalryman named Byrd C. Willis. "We captured three negro soldiers the first we had seen. They were taken out on the road side and shot, & their bodies left there."[6]

Though kept apart from the major fighting of the Overland Campaign, black soldiers found validation through their participation. Writing to the *Christian Recorder* from Hanover, Virginia, on June 8, Sergeant Brock of the Forty-third U.S.C.T. explained, "We have been instrumental in liberating some five hundred of our sisters and brothers from the accursed yoke of human bondage. You see them coming in every direction, some in carts, some on their masters' horses, and great numbers on foot, carrying their bundles on their heads. They manifest their love of liberty by every possible emotion. As several of them remarked to me, it seemed to them like heaven, so greatly did they realize the difference between slavery and freedom."[7]

A writer for the *Philadelphia Press* claimed that the black troops in the Overland Campaign "were invariably selected to bring up the rear of the Army of the Potomac, because of their known disinclination for straggling." Yet a glance through the Regimental Order Book of the Forty-third U.S.C.T. suggests otherwise. From Colonel Sigfried's headquarters on May 24 came General Orders No. 3, exhorting his officers to insure that "the troops in their commands do not straggle on the march." On May 26, Edward Ferrero issued his General Orders No. 11 against the "frequent acts of vandalism... perpetuated by stragglers and followers of this army." More persuasive for obedience, perhaps, was the fate of black stragglers who were captured.[8]

It was in the latter part of the Overland Campaign, on May 24, that the Ninth Corps was formally assigned to the Army of the Potomac. On June 13, the Federals marched to the James River, which was crossed on June 14 and 15. The target was now Petersburg. Attacks made on June 15 (principally by black troops from the Army of the James) seized a portion of Petersburg's outer defenses. However, follow-up efforts on June 16, 17, and 18 (principally by white troops from the Army of the Potomac) failed to occupy the city. The operation now became a siege.

Despite wearing a U.S. uniform and carrying a gun, life for the black soldiers in the Army of the Potomac was a constant series of racist confrontations. "We lay there subjected to the prejudice of the white troops," wrote a soldier in the Thirty-ninth U.S.C.T. of service in the Petersburg trenches. In some cases, it seemed as if the white men commanding the U.S.C.T. regiments actually feared the African Americans in the same way that slave owners feared their human chattel. When punishment was meted out to black men in uniform it could be brutal. At the end of June, an officer in one of Burnside's black regiments noted in his diary, "A sad affair occurred in Co. 'G' while we were on the march, one of his men refused [to] obey some order of the Capt. when he shot him so that he died in a few moments." "The conduct of the officers toward the soldiers is good only at times," complained a soldier in the Forty-third U.S.C.T. "Some of them do things which I think they have no right to do."[9]

While the deadly routine of duty in the trenches and the unceasing labors under a hot July sun began to sap the spirit of the white troops, those in the U.S.C.T. units understood the significance of their presence. "We have seen the fruits of slavery," wrote David R. Brown of the Thirty-first U.S.C.T. on July 18, "the desolation and despair of hundreds rushing into our lines, crying and praying for protection." "We know, and the slave knows," added Alexander Banks of that regiment, "that fighting for the Union is fighting against slavery."[10]

The initial assignments for the black soldiers of Ferrero's Ninth Corps division were largely laboring ones. "We have been marching for the last two weeks from one part to another along the front," Sergeant Brock wrote on July 16, "engaged in picket and fatigue duty. Our division has built two immense forts, connected by a long chain of breastworks. Sometimes they were in the trenches, in very dangerous places, the bullets whistling over and among our troops all day and all night long, while the men were engaged in digging."[11]

While the sergeant was finishing his letter, other Union soldiers were resting on their picks and shovels after one of the most remarkable military engineering achievements of the war. At a point where the siege lines were especially close, resourceful white troops serving in the Ninth Corps had secretly burrowed a mine under the Rebel position known as Elliott's Salient. Work began on June 25, and on July 27 the Ninth Corp troops packed the mine that ran parallel to the enemy entrenchments with four tons of gunpowder.

Even while the tunneling took place, Ambrose Burnside pondered the military question. As he later testified to a congressional committee, "During the month of July...I had made up my mind, in case an assault was to be made by the 9th corps, to put [the black]...division in the advance." In other comments regarding this affair, Burnside enumerated his reasons, "inasmuch as that division had not suffered so severely [as the three white divisions], in fact had not been in any general engagement during the campaign, but had frequently been very honorably engaged on the outposts of the army. General Ferrero himself and all his officers expressed to me their utmost confidence in his troops, and especially his confidence in their ability to make a charge, or in other words a dash."[12]

Testifying before the same group of congressmen, Ferrero described the plan approved by Burnside. "The mine was under a considerable fort upon the right. There was a small fort, a short distance, probably six hundred yards to the left, with three or four guns. My idea was to make an assault at the moment of the explosion of the mine between these two points. I wanted to advance one brigade, which was to be the leading brigade, then divide it in two parts, one portion to go to the right and sweep the enemy's lines in that direction, and the other portion to go down the left and sweep the lines in that direction. The other [brigade]...of the division [was]...to march forward in column, and carry the crest of Cemetery Hill."[13]

The commander of Ferrero's Second Brigade, Henry G. Thomas, was especially attentive to his men as they prepared for their first major action. He wrote:

Any striking event or piece of news was usually eagerly discussed by the white troops....Not so with the blacks; important news such as that before us, after the bare announcement, was usually followed by long silence. They sat about in groups, "studying," as they called it. They waited, like the Quakers, for the spirit to move; when the spirit moved, one of their singers would uplift a mighty voice, like a bard of old, in a wild sort of chant. If he did not strike a sympathetic chord in his hearers . . . he would sing it again and again, altering sometimes the words, more often the music. If his changes met general acceptance, one voice after another would chime in; . . . and the song would become the song of the command.

The night we learned that we were to lead the charge the [men] . . . formed circles in their company streets and were sitting on the ground intently and solemnly "studying." At last a heavy voice began to sing,

> We-e looks li-ike me-en a-a-marchin' on,
> We looks li-ike men-er-war."[14]

No specific date had been set for exploding the mine, but events soon transpired to make it July 30. Burnside's real problems began on July 28 when he told George Meade's headquarters that the mine was set to go and was informed that General Meade opposed his plan to let the black troops lead the attack. As Meade later explained, " '[Burnside's] colored division [was] . . . a new division, and had never been under fire—had never been tried—and as this was an operation which I knew beforehand was one requiring the best troops, I thought it impolitic to trust it." Meade also wanted the first units over the top to press straight on to Cemetery Hill, instead of fanning left and right as Burnside intended.[15]

After arguing his case with Meade, who finally promised to lay the entire matter before U. S. Grant, Burnside went back to his headquarters and waited. By now the time for exploding the gunpowder had been set for 3:30 AM July 30, so the clock was ticking. At midday July 29, Burnside was in conference with the commanders of his three white divisions when Meade arrived with members of his staff. Grant had sustained Meade, Burnside was told. The black troops would not lead the attack.

All of Burnside's careful planning collapsed like a house of cards. The assault was on, so it remained to decide which of the white divisions would go first. In a fit of desperation, he had the three

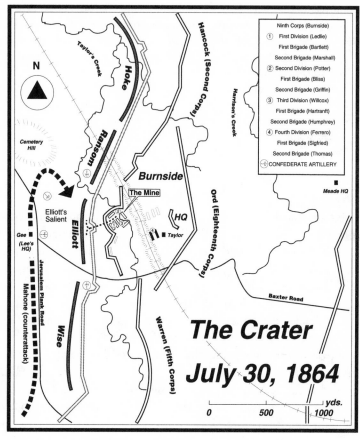

Map by Noah Andre Trudeau

commanders draw lots from a hat. In this way, Burnside's First Division, commanded by Brigadier General James H. Ledlie, was selected to spearhead the assault. A new plan was improvised; the First Division would dash around the crater caused by the explosion to seize Cemetery Hill, the Third Division (Brigadier General Orlando B. Willcox) would cross behind Ledlie to form a defensive line to the left, while the Second Division (Brigadier General Robert B. Potter) would do likewise on the right. Only then would Ferrero's men come forward to sweep into Petersburg.

Soon after dark July 29, the Ninth Corps troops began filing into their jump-off positions. The black soldiers massed on the open hillside below the ruins of the Taylor house, not far from an entrance to one of the principal deep-approach trenches, known as covered ways. "Around us could be heard the shuffling tread of troops, but it was so dark that nothing could be seen," recalled Lieutenant Freeman S. Bowley of the Thirtieth U.S.C.T. (Sigfried's brigade). "Down on the picket line the rifles were flashing, and over head the bullets hummed with that peculiar droning sound of the nearly spent bullet. Most of us went to sleep as soon as we halted." In the Twenty-seventh U.S.C.T. (Sigfried), Sergeant James H. Payne held an impromptu sacred service. "Many professors [of religion] appeared to be greatly stirred up," he recalled, "while sinners seemed to be deeply touched and aroused to a sense of their danger and duty. Our prayer meeting was short but not without good and lasting impressions being made upon the hearts and minds of many."[16]

"Before day we were up and ready," remembered Lieutenant Fred A. Chapman in the Twenty-ninth U.S.C.T. (Thomas's brigade). "Every one felt the danger awaiting him, and there was unusual silence. All seemed occupied with their own thoughts." There were problems igniting the powder in the mine and nearly an hour and fifteen minutes after it was scheduled to blow, the fuse flame finally met the explosive. Chaplain Garland H. White, an ex-slave himself, was moving among his flock in the Twenty-eighth U.S.C.T. (Thomas's brigade) as the explosion went off. "Just at this junction the earth began to shake," he wrote afterwards, "as though the hand of God intended a reversal of the laws of nature." The experience was more vivid for Captain Warren H. Hurd of the Twenty-third U.S.C.T., who watched in awe as a "large black cloud ... appeared to rise out of the ground." Lieutenant Bowley remembered first a "jar of the earth under our feet," followed by a "terrible rumbling."[17]

Where there had been a redoubt and trenches holding three hundred men, four cannon, and thirty gunners, there was now a great smoking cavity, 150 to 200 feet in length, sixty feet in width, and some thirty feet deep. Cued by the explosion, 110 Federal cannon and fifty-four mortars opened fire along nearly two miles of trench lines. This cannonade, declared Lieutenant Bowley, "was one of the most terrific of the war." It was all too much for Private Miles Keyes in the Twenty-eighth U.S.C.T. This was the cause later given by his comrades for Keyes's contracting an "unsoundness of mind" that would end his days in a lunatic asylum near Cincinnati.[18]

About five minutes after the debris stopped raining down, James H. Ledlie ordered his division to advance, and then retired to a nearby aid station for a drink. Here he would remain, with an occasional foray to observe what was happening around the crater, for the rest of the battle. No part of the hurriedly cobbled together battle plan was successfully executed. Within ninety minutes the operations was a shambles. Back where the black troops waited for the order to advance, the soldiers got ready. Chaplain White was suddenly besieged by men asking him to write their loved ones and begging him "when pay-day comes, if it ever does come, send what money is due [home]."[19]

"It seemed [to take] forever [to move forward]," wrote Lieutenant Hurd of the Twenty-third U.S.C.T. "The whole [division]... filed through a single parallel.... We were hindered by officers and orderlies coming to the rear, the parallel being only about six feet wide." A staff officer Edward Ferrero had sent ahead to scout the situation returned with a frightening description of the chaos awaiting. Ferrero appealed his orders to one of Burnside's staff, who told Ferrero to halt his men while the directives were confirmed. The officer quickly returned and, as Ferrero recalled, "reported that the order was peremptory for me to carry my division through at all hazards." With the Thirtieth U.S.C.T. leading, the troops of Sigfried's brigade began to move from the Union trenches across the no-man's-land toward the crater.[20]

"The appearance of the regimental colors seemed to be the signal for the enemy's batteries, and it was volley after volley of canister and shrapnel they gave us," said Colonel Delevan Bates of the Thirtieth. "Down went our flag," recalled Lieutenant Bowley, "the color-sergeant staining the stars and stripes with his blood." Behind the regiment the rest of the brigade spilled out into the killing ground; the Forty-third, then the Thirty-ninth, and finally the Twenty-seventh U.S.C.T. "Did they flinch or hang back?" a member of the Twenty-seventh asked newspaper readers rhetorically. "No; they went forward with undaunted bravery!"[21]

Colonel Bates tried to lead his men around to the right of the crater, but enemy fire pressed the head of his column into the pit. "Push down the line," Bates called out to Captain David E. Proctor, in charge of the leading company. Proctor and his men rushed through the crater and out the other side where a rough line of battle was formed. Behind them, the Forty-third U.S.C.T. also stumbled into the smoking hole, and Lieutenant Colonel Hall saw at once that the mob made following the Thirtieth impossible. The enemy still held trenches close to the right, but Hall spotted what he believed was a partially sheltered route to attack them. He personally led his men "along the front of the enemy's intrenchments, so close that some of my officers and men were wounded by the bayonets, others burned by the powder flashes of the foe." Once his regiment was aligned, Hall (soon to be wounded) ordered a charge that plunged his black soldiers into hand-to-hand combat. "The men killed numbers of the enemy in spite of the efforts of their officers to restrain them," Hall wrote, "and we took prisoners in these intrenchments." The Forty-third linked up with the Thirtieth on the outside slope of the crater, where they were joined by what remained of Sigfried's brigade.[22]

It took Ferrero's First Brigade about a half hour to unclog the passageway so that Colonel Thomas could follow. The Thirty-first U.S.C.T. was first to rush into the open ground between the lines, followed by the others with the Nineteenth U.S.C.T. trailing last. "They did their duty and that bravely," said David R. Brown of the Thirty-first. "While in this work and coming through we were exposed to a heavy cross fire of artillery & musketry," recalled Captain Robert Porter of the Twenty-ninth U.S.C.T. "Here we lost all our line officers." From his place back at the main trench line, Chaplain White watched the regimental flag go up and into the enemy's works. "Boys," he cheered to those nearby, "the day is ours, and Petersburg is sure."[23]

Henry G. Thomas never had full control of his brigade; two of his regiments got stuck in the confusion of the crater, while one, the Nineteenth U.S.C.T., was hung up before entering the pit. Thomas tried to lead the Thirty-first U.S.C.T. in a charge but these soldiers wouldn't move out of the great hole. Their commander, Lieutenant Colonel William E. W. Ross, was hit, along with many of his officers. One of his orderlies, Lieutenant Christopher Pennell, grabbed the brigade guidon and stood at the lip of the pit calling for the men to follow him. "In a moment," Thomas wrote, "a musketry fire was focused upon him, whirling him round and round several times before he fell."[24]

"Bullets came through all the little alleyways, and found victims in the most unexpected places," said Lieutenant Bowley. At one point the regimental flag of the Thirtieth U.S.C.T. was picked up by Private William Gray who was then "struck by a minie ball in the left breast causing almost immediately death." One officer not present to see any of this was Edward Ferrero who remained back at the Union jump-off trench. His principal contribution to the events that were unfolding came soon after 8:00 AM., when he sent a aide forward with orders for Sigfried and Thomas to follow their original instructions to advance to the Jerusalem Plank Road and Cemetery Hill.[25]

Somehow the two pulled enough of their men together to make the effort. The thin black lines were dressed under fire and the order to advance was given. As the uneven files lurched ahead some white units joined the attempt. More than three hours had passed since the gunpowder galleries had been ignited. In what proved to be perhaps the greatest failure of this entire operation, the Union Fifth Corps, supporting the Ninth on its left, did not mount enough pressure to prevent Robert E. Lee from shifting three brigades in that sector to counterattack at the center. When the black and white Union battle line began moving forward, it was hit by Confederate troops who had marched up from positions south of the breach, to the accompaniment of stories that the U.S.C.T. soldiers were giving no quarter. Everything dissolved into a wild melee.

Lieutenant Bowley watched in horror as the black battle lines bent under the onslaught, then shattered. "For a moment the men moved backward, to the left, firing as they retreated; then the enemy charged with a yell, and poured a volley into their very faces. Instantly the whole body broke, went over the breastworks toward the Union line, or ran down the trenches towards the crater."[26]

This was the end of Ferrero's division as a cohesive fighting force in this battle. "My troops came back in very bad order," he later testified. Private Leonard Carter of the Twenty-eighth U.S.C.T. was a bit closer to the action than Ferrero. He remembered that the "confusion became such that officers were separated from their commands, and comrades from each other." Because few of the white men present truly expected that the black troops would prove themselves in combat, the retreat of Ferrero's division became the one incident often identified as the reason for the failure this day. In defense of the black troops, one of the U.S.C.T. officers described their ordeal, standing exposed under the enemy's heavy fire "with no attempt at order or organization in either command [Sigfried's or Thomas's], and with panic stricken [white] men spreading alarm as they flew to the rear, our men, who were in their first engagement, became wild, confused, terror stricken, and, with the veterans of a score of battles, ran, like the whole army, including myself, at the first Bull Run.... The charge of cowardice can not be proven against our officers or men, without bringing to lasting disgrace the whole force engaged."[27]

By 10:00 AM, the entire Union breakthrough had been reduced to about a thousand disorganized men, black and white, trapped in the crater or in the earthworks immediately adjacent to it. For the moment the Confederates (whose fierce counterattacks had cost them dearly) lacked sufficient manpower for a final push. As they built up strength for that purpose, they subjected the crater to a pitiless barrage of mortar and artillery shells, while snipers targeted anyone who showed himself or tried to run back to the Union lines. "My brain reels, and my soul recoils with horror whenever I have occasion to speak of what I saw on that dreadful day," recollected a soldier in the Thirty-first U.S.C.T.[28]

Lieutenant Bowley was among those who huddled in the crater. He remembered that the "men were dropping thick and fast, most of them shot through the head. Every man that was shot rolled down the steep sides to the bottom, and in places they were piled up four and five deep." By 11:00 AM, any hope of expanding the assault was gone. The situation within the crater now crossed the line from combat to something far worse. In the words of John W. Pratt of the Thirtieth U.S.C.T., "We say slaughter for we can call it nothing else—nor can any one who was present say truthfully that it was not." In a bitter harvest of the racism prevalent throughout the Union ranks, a new horror was inflicted on the black troops caught in the disaster. "It was believed among the whites that the enemy would give no quarter to negroes, or to the whites taken with them, and so to be shut up with blacks in the crater was equal to a doom of death," recalled a New York soldier present. "It has been positively asserted that white men bayoneted blacks who fell back into the crater. This was in order to preserve the whites from Confederate vengeance."[29]

It was around 2:00 PM before the Rebels had amassed enough troops to storm the crater. These soldiers from Virginia, Georgia, North Carolina, Alabama, and South Carolina swarmed to the edge of the pit and then down into it. Now the pure killing began. "Within... ten minutes," recalled a Virginia soldier, "the whole floor of the trench was strewn with the dead bodies of negroes, in some places in such numbers that it was difficult to make one's way along the trench without stepping on them." "As soon as we got upon them, they threw down their arms to surrender, but were not allowed to do so," said an artilleryman in a letter written right after the battle. "I think over two hundred negroes got into our lines, by surrendering & running in, along with the whites, while the fighting was going on. I don't believe that much over half of these ever reached the rear."[30]

Private Isaac Gaskin of the Twenty-ninth U.S.C.T. was one of the "lucky" ones. "After I was made a prisoner," he recalled, "I was shot at by a rebel guard and my cartridge box entirely carried away and my hip severely injured. Just before firing at me he, with an oath, called me a damn nigger, and said if he had known I was a nigger he would have never taken me prisoner, but that I had so much of that damn Yankee blood over my face that he couldn't tell what I was. He said he did not recognize any damn negro as a prisoner of war and that I would never get back to my brother Yankees alive."[31]

Those blacks who managed to get taken alive were corralled in a ravine in the rear of the Rebel lines. Some of their white officers, fearing Southern retribution, tore off their unit insignias and denied any association with them. When Lieutenant Bowley's turn came, he thought of the "black men who had rallied with me in the Crater, and who had died to the last man. Then I told my comrades that I should face the music, and if I died, I should die without denying the brave fellows we had left behind in that trap of death. One of my comrades . . . said, 'I'm with you!' and when our names and rank were taken down, we said, 'Thirtieth United States Colored Infantry!' and saw the words 'negro officer' written opposite our names on the list."[32]

Union losses in this battle were horrendous. Of approximately fifteen thousand men engaged in the Ninth Corps, 3,475 were casualties. More were killed, wounded, or missing in the black division than any of the white ones, even though they had been fighting for fully ninety minutes before the U.S.C.T. units went in. The official tally of those killed or mortally wounded in Ferrero's division was 209, but a careful examination of pension files and compiled service records shows that an additional 227 of those previously listed as missing either died in the fighting or right afterward. Of the 4,500 blacks who battled at the Crater, 1,327 were hit or injured in some way. Many of the wounded were transported to City Point, where a nurse named Helen Gilson had established a Colored Hospital Service.

It took nearly twenty-four hours for both sides of the machinery of military protocol to agree upon a truce to bury the dead and succor the wounded. A surprisingly high proportion of the wounded who were found were black, perhaps because they recognized the danger of seeking help within the Rebel lines. Among the dead who were identified and buried this day was Henry Heighton, a private in the Twenty-ninth U.S.C.T. Just two weeks earlier he and his wife had exchanged letters. "I feel I am as much enlist[ed] in prayer as ever," Susannah Heighton wrote on July 11, "even more so for I pray for you daily & hourly and hope you will do the same for your self." In his reply, written July 19, Henry Heighton informed his wife that for "some time I have not been very well, but feel right smart at present." He went on to say, "Remember me . . . that my return may be safe to the bosom of loved ones and that I may be kept in the path of duty and not be led astray by the many snares that beset the path of the soldier in the field." On August 1, Sergeant Charles Greenwell of Company B, helped bury his friend, Henry Heighton.[33]

Sergeant Payne of the Twenty-seventh U.S.C.T. had some comments for the readers of the *Christian Recorder* about the battle and the fate of blacks taken prisoner. "Instead of a general effort being made, as was contemplated," he said, "only a few men were taken in to be slaughtered and taken prisoner, which is the equivalent to death, for no mercy is shown to them when captured, although some still plead that the rebels are treating the colored prisoners very well; but before I can be convinced that this is so, I wish to hear one of the prisoners tell the story." One who did tell his story after the war was Sergeant Rodney Long of the Twenty-ninth U.S.C.T. Captured at the Crater, he wound up spending seven months in Confederate detention at Danville. "We suffered terribly while in prison," he recalled in 1886, "and most of our men died there." Isaac Gaskin, who survived capture because his bloody face passed him as white, also went to Danville. "I was punished severely on account of my color," he said. "Out of 180 colored prisoners taken, only seven survived."[34]

A total of twenty-four Medals of Honor were later awarded to men who fought at the Crater, four to individuals from Ferrero's division: three white officers and one black enlisted man. Sergeant Decatur Dorsey, of the Thirty-ninth U.S.C.T., was honored for leading his men forward and then helping to rally them after the retreat. There were black heroes aplenty for a survivor of the Thirty-first U.S.C.T., who never forgot this day "when the colored soldiers won a name that can never be blotted from the pages of the nation's history."[35]

The findings of a military court of inquiry held in the month of August resulted in Burnside's removal from command of the Ninth Corps. First Division commander Ledlie suffered a similar fate, while mild reprimands were meted out to division commanders Willcox and Ferrero. "None of the troops, white or colored, are responsible for the action of the Generals," said Chaplain White. "I hold that there can be no higher sin in all the world than to blame innocent people for the consequences for which they are not responsible. I care not who it is, whether king or subject, General or private, it makes no difference with me in a point of exposition of truth."[36]

Henry G. Thomas was witness to another piece of this battle's aftermath. After noting the song that his black soldiers sang before the fight, Thomas continued, "Until we fought the battle of the crater they sang this every night to the exclusion of all other songs. After that defeat, they sang it no more."[37]

The last major operation at Petersburg to involve the Army of the Potomac's black division took place in late October. The Confederate lines covered the southern side of the city, then hinged to the southwest, so as to protect the vital Boydton Plank Road to the point where it crossed a stream known as Hatcher's Run. To tackle this flank, the Federals employed three infantry corps, plus almost all the available cavalry. The plan developed by Major General Meade had the Ninth Corps striking the Rebel lines near the hinge to develop the strength of the position and, if possible, to break through.

The Ninth Corps entered this fight still the only one in the Army of the Potomac with black units in it. Burnside was long gone, Major General John G. Parke now commanded. Edward Ferrero, seemingly no worse for wear over the Crater fiasco, was in charge of the black division, which consisted of a First Brigade under Colonel Delevan Bates and a Second Brigade under Colonel Henry G. Thomas. The part played by these units is best described in a letter written right afterward by Sergeant Brock of the Forty-third U.S.C.T. (Bates's brigade):

On last Tuesday [October 25] we were ordered to take six days' rations, three in our knapsacks and three in our haversacks. On the same afternoon I saw that each man had the provisions ordered. Every one thought that a move would be made immediately. All night, Tuesday, every ear was on the qui viva to hear the order to move, but no order came.... On Wednesday evening we went to bed as usual. At two o'clock on Thursday morning a single horseman rode into camp, with a despatch to our commander. Every man was ordered to strike his tent and get ready to march immediately. Soon afterwards long columns of troops commenced to march out past our camp.—In about ten minutes every man was ready to march. But the order to move had not yet arrived, we lay there till broad daylight, before we moved....

At last, after many hours delay, the order was given to move forward. The whole division was soon in motion. The first brigade leading. We proceeded along slowly and cautiously about a mile before we met any sign of the enemy.... Our brigade advanced in gallant style, driving the rebels before them all day. Towards night the enemy fell back to his works, where he was found to be strongly fortified. Our boys built breastworks along their line while our skirmishers were busily engaged in watching the enemy....

On Thursday night [October 27] it commenced to rain, and the boys had to take it rough and ready, without tents all night, next morning many of them were dripping wet. Soon after dark, on Thursday night, the rebels attempted to surprise us, but we were not to be caught napping. They found the boys ready and waiting to welcome them with hospitable hands to bloody graves.

On Friday morning [October 28] every one thought that the order of the day would be an attempt to make still further advances, but contrary to every one's expectations we were ordered to fall back. The Second Corps fell back from their position early in the morning, we following soon afterwards.

Now we are in our old camp, where we started from. What good we accomplished we have yet to learn.[38]

In this operation, known both as "Boydton Plank Road" and "Hatcher's Run," Ferrero's division lost seven, who were killed; sixty-seven, who were wounded; and six, who were missing. The greatest losses were in Sergeant Brock's regiment, which suffered all the killed, nineteen of the wounded, and four of the missing. The operation itself was barren of results.

The October 27 action, marking the last offensive movement for the black troops north of the James, was also their final operation within an integrated corps. In November, U. S. Grant, responded favorably to a suggestion from Major General Benjamin F. Butler to consolidate all black units into the Army of the James. The U.S.C.T. regiments assigned to the Ninth Corps were placed under Butler's control, followed, on December 3, by the creation of the all-black Twenty-fifth Corps, Army of the James, the only such command in the annals of American military history. (At the same time, most of the white troops in the Army of the James were put into another new organization, the Twenty-fourth Corps.)

Thus ended the great experiment. Outside the community of African American soldiers, the results were decidedly mixed. In the period from May to December, the black soldiers operating as part of the Army of the Potomac had marched and fought to a degree unparalleled by any other African American unit. On the surface little seems to have been proven by this service, for neither Grant nor Meade mention it. Reflecting back on the Overland Campaign, a member of the all-white Second Corps admitted that he and his comrades "used to . . . ill treat every negro, soldier or slave, that we passed." For a white Massachusetts man in the Ninth Corps the integration case had definitely not been proven. "I am willing the niggers should fight but I say put them all in together and let them fight," he declared. "If not, keep them out and let the white man do it." A New York comrade was even more adamant that the Crater experience had shown these troops to be untrustworthy. "I say put the niggers out of our corps as I do not want to be in the corps they are," he proclaimed.[39]

Others were more willing to let the deeds speak without bias attached. A New Jersey man in the Ninth Corps wrote that "when I was home I used to run down colored troops as bad as any one, but one month in Virginia has entirely cured me of that as they did all the fighting in our Corps and fought well." A Gettysburg veteran of a famous unit made up of western regiments found the soldiers of the black division to be "reliable men who possess the courage and the ability to meet any danger on the shortest possible notice.... When in the field with the old Iron Brigade I never felt one whit safer than I did with the regiments of the Black Division."[40]

The experience of fighting with the Army of the Potomac was central to what the black community hoped would be a transformation of American society. "No longer can it be said that we have no rights in the country in which we live because we have never marched forward to its defense," proclaimed Sergeant Brock of the Forty-third U.S.C.T. "I can have the satisfaction of saying I helped sustain the nation's pride," added a comrade in the Thirty-first U.S.C.T. The matter was clear for Chaplain White of the Twenty-eighth U.S.C.T. "We left our wives and little ones to follow the stars and stripes ... with a determination never to turn back until it should be proclaimed from Washington that the flag of the Union waves over a nation of freemen," he said. "The historian's pen cannot fail to locate us somewhere among the good and great, who have fought and bled upon the altar of their country."[41]

6

"The Tocsin of Freedom":
The Black Leadership
of Radical Reconstruction

ERIC FONER

RECONSTRUCTION, the turbulent period that followed the Civil War, was a time of momentous changes in American political and social life. But no development during that era marked so dramatic a break with the nation's traditions, or aroused such bitter hostility from Reconstruction's opponents, as the appearance of large numbers of black Americans in public office only a few years after the destruction of slavery.

Before the Civil War, blacks did not form part of America's "political nation." In 1860, only five Northern states, all with tiny black populations, allowed black men to vote on the same terms as white. Black officeholding was unknown in the slave South and virtually unheard of in the free states as well. During Presidential Reconstruction (1865–67), voting and elective office in the South continued to be restricted to whites. Black officeholding began in earnest in 1867, when Congress ordered the election of new Southern governments under suffrage rules that did not discriminate on the basis of race. By 1877, when the last radical Reconstruction governments were overthrown, around two thousand black men had held federal, state, and local public offices, ranging from member of Congress to justice of the peace. Although much reduced after the abandonment of Reconstruction, black officeholding continued until the turn of the century, when most Southern blacks were disenfranchised, and, in a few places, even beyond that time. Not until the passage of the Voting Rights Act of 1965 did significant numbers of black Southerners again hold public office.

To Reconstruction's opponents, black officeholding symbolized the fatal "error" of national policy after the Civil War—the effort to elevate former slaves to a status for which they were utterly unprepared and congenitally incompetent. The Democratic press described constitutional conventions and legislatures with black members as "menageries" and "monkey houses," and ridiculed the former slaves who considered themselves "as competent to frame a code of laws as Lycurgus." They portrayed black officials as ignorant and propertyless, lacking both the education and the economic stake in society supposedly necessary for intelligent governance.[1] After Reconstruction ended, some of its opponents tried to erase black officials from the historical record altogether. Soon after Democrats regained control of Georgia, Alexander St. Clair Abrams, who compiled the state's legislative manual, decided to omit black lawmakers from the volume's biographical sketches. It would be absurd, he wrote, to record "the lives of men who were but yesterday our slaves, and whose past careers, probably, embraced such menial occupations as boot-blacking, shaving, table-waiting, and the like."[2]

These contemporary views were elaborated by the anti-Reconstruction historians whose works shaped public and scholarly perceptions of the era for much of this century. In popular representations such as D. W. Griffith's film *Birth of a Nation*, Claude G. Bowers's sensationalized best seller *The Tragic Era* (which described Louisiana's Reconstruction legislature as "a zoo"), the alleged incompetence of black officeholders and the horrors of "Negro rule" justified Reconstruction's violent overthrow and Northern acquiescence in the South's nullification of the Fourteenth and Fifteenth Amendments. As late as 1968, E. Merton Coulter, the last wholly antagonistic scholar of the era, described Georgia's most prominent Reconstruction black officials as swindlers and "scamps," and suggested that whatever positive qualities they possessed were inherited from white ancestors.[3]

The task of offering a more sympathetic and nuanced portrait of black officeholders began early in this century, when surviving veterans of the era like John R. Lynch, black scholars such as Alrutheus A. Taylor and W. E. B. Du Bois, and white historians like T. Harry Williams challenged the dominant interpretation. Not until the 1960s, however, did revisionism, inspired by the civil rights revolution, sweep over the field, irrevocably laying to rest the earlier viewpoint and producing a host of important new studies of Reconstruction at the state and national levels. Today, not only has the history of the era been rewritten completely, but most scholars view Reconstruction as a laudable, though flawed, effort to create a functioning interracial democracy for the first time in American history and view Reconstruction's overthrow as a tragedy that powerfully affected the subsequent course of American development.[4]

Thanks to the past generation's Reconstruction scholarship, the information available on black officeholders has expanded enormously. Nonetheless, the lives of most black officials have remained shrouded in obscurity. Many disappear entirely from the historical record after leaving public office. Over the past several years, as an outgrowth of my research on Reconstruction, I have assembled biographical information for about 1,465 of the era's black officials. The results have been published by Oxford University Press in a biographical directory, *Freedom's Lawmakers*. In this essay, I draw upon my findings to offer a portrait of the era's black political leadership and introduce you to some of these remarkable individuals.

Although blacks held office in every part of the old Confederacy during Reconstruction (as well as in Missouri and the nation's capital), the number varied considerably from state to state. Clearly, the size of the state's black population helped to determine the extent of black officeholding. Thus, it is not surprising that South Carolina, Mississippi, and Louisiana had the largest number of black officeholders. South Carolina was the only state where blacks comprised a majority of the House of Representatives throughout Reconstruction, and about half the state Senate between 1872 and 1876. South Carolina and Louisiana, in addition, possessed large communities of free blacks, many of them educated, economically independent, and well positioned to demand a role in government from the outset of Reconstruction.

To the black percentage of the voting population, however, other factors must be added that help explain the pattern of black officeholding, including the length of time that Reconstruction survived, attitudes of white Republicans toward blacks exercising political power, and the structure of state and local government. Republican leaders in Florida and Georgia, bent on attracting white voters to their party by limiting the number of black officials, framed constitutions with legislative apportionments biased against black counties, and in which many state and local offices were filled by appointment rather than election. In North Carolina, by contrast, where blacks were far from a majority of the population, the new constitution democratized local government, allowing black voters in plantation counties to choose their own officials.

Nowhere in the South did blacks control the workings of state government, and nowhere did they hold office in numbers commensurate with their proportion of the total population, not to mention the Republican electorate. The old idea of Reconstruction as an era of "black supremacy" has long since been discarded as a myth. Nonetheless, the fact that more than fourteen hundred blacks occupied positions of political authority in the South represented a stunning departure in American government. Moreover, because of the black population's concentration, nearly all these officials served in or represented plantation counties, home of the wealthiest and, before the Civil War, most powerful Southerners. The spectacle of former slaves representing the South Carolina rice kingdom and the Mississippi cotton belt in state legislatures, assessing taxes on the property of their former owners, and serving on juries alongside them epitomized the political revolution wrought by Reconstruction.

At every level of government, federal, state, and local, blacks were represented in government during Reconstruction. Two sat in the United States Senate (Hiram Revels and Blanche K. Bruce of Mississippi) and fourteen in the House of Representatives. Blacks also held numerous federal patronage appointments, including postmaster, deputy U.S. marshal, treasury agent, and clerks in federal offices. At least forty blacks held positions in custom houses, most in Charleston and New Orleans.[5]

In December 1872, P. B. S. Pinchback became governor of Louisiana when he succeeded Henry C. Warmoth, who had been suspended because of impeachment proceedings. Pinchback served until the inauguration five weeks later of William P. Kellogg; a century and a quarter would pass until L. Douglas Wilder of Virginia, elected in 1989, became the next black American to serve as governor. Twenty-five major state executive positions (lieutenant governor, treasurer, superintendent of education, secretary of state, and state commissioner) were occupied by blacks during Reconstruction, and one, Jonathan J. Wright of South Carolina, sat on a state supreme court. And during Reconstruction, 683 black men sat in the lower house of state legislatures (four serving as Speaker of the House), and 112 in state senates.

In virtually every county with a sizable black population, blacks held some local office during Reconstruction. At least 111 served as members of the boards that governed county affairs, variously called the county commission, board of supervisors, board of police, and police jury. There were at least forty-one black sheriffs (most in Louisiana and Mississippi), and twenty-five deputy sheriffs. Five held the office of mayor, and 132 served on city councils and boards of aldermen (with sizable representations in communities from Petersburg to Little Rock).

The backgrounds of the black officials reflect the often-neglected diversity of the black population in mid-nineteenth-century America. Nearly half of those for whom information is available had been born free, and fifty-four were former slaves who gained their liberty before the Civil War, by manumission, purchase, or escaping to the North. Fewer than three hundred thousand free blacks lived in the South in 1860, but they clearly enjoyed far greater opportunities to obtain an education, accumulate property, and observe public affairs than did most slaves. Half the officeholders known to have been free served in South Carolina and Louisiana. Virginia was another state with a large free black community, whose origins dated back to the colonial period and the large-scale manumissions of the Revolutionary era. Here too, well over half the black officeholders had been free before the war.

Many of the freeborn officeholders were men of uncommon backgrounds and abilities. Ovid Gregory of Alabama, a member of the constitutional convention and legislature, was fluent in Spanish and French and had traveled widely in the United States and Latin America before the Civil War. James H. Jones, deputy sheriff of Wake County, North Carolina, had worked as coachman and personal servant for Jefferson Davis during the Civil War. Jones helped the Confederate president escape from Richmond in April 1865, and three decades later drove the funeral car when Davis's body was interred in a Virginia cemetery.

Many freeborn officeholders held themselves aloof from the plight of slaves before the Civil War. Twenty-two had themselves been slaveholders, nearly all in South Carolina and Louisiana. A few held slaves by necessity, owning a relative who, according to state law, could not be freed without being compelled to leave the state. Others were craftsmen whose slaves worked in their shops or entrepreneurs who purchased slaves as an investment, and one, Antoine Dubuclet, subsequently Louisiana's Reconstruction treasurer, was a sugar planter who owned over one hundred slaves in 1860.

On the other hand, a number of free black officials had placed themselves in considerable danger before the war by offering clandestine assistance to slaves. James D. Porter, a member of Georgia's legislature during Reconstruction, had operated secret schools for black children in Charleston and Savannah. William Hodges, who served as superintendent of the poor for Norfolk County during Reconstruction, had been arrested around 1830 for providing slaves with forged free papers, leading to the persecution of his entire family and their flight to the North. William's brother Willis, a constitutional convention delegate, described free blacks and slaves as "one man of sorrow."

No fewer than 138 officeholders lived outside the South before the Civil War. Most were born in the North (where about two hundred twenty thousand free blacks lived in 1860), but their numbers also included free Southerners whose families moved to the North, free blacks and a few privileged slaves sent North for education, several immigrants from abroad, and fugitives from bondage. Although these black "carpetbaggers" have received far less attention from historians than their white counterparts, they included some of the era's most prominent lawmakers, and individuals with remarkable life histories. Mifflin Gibbs, a native of Philadelphia, traveled to California in 1850 as part of the gold rush, established the state's first black newspaper, moved to British Columbia in 1858 to engage in railroad and mining ventures, and eventually made his way to Arkansas, where he became a judge, attorney, and longtime power in the Republican party. Joseph T. Wilson, a customs inspector at Norfolk, had worked on a whaling ship in the Pacific Ocean, and T. Morris Chester, appointed a district superintendent of education during Louisiana's Reconstruction, had lived in Liberia and Great Britain and visited Russia and France.

Ten black officials are known to have escaped from slavery before the Civil War. Half had been born in Virginia, whose proximity to the North made flight far easier than from the Deep South. Daniel M. Norton, who had escaped from Virginia around 1850, returned to the Hampton area in 1864. The following year, he was "elected" as local blacks' representative on a Freedmen's Bureau court, but was denied his place by the bureau. Embittered by this experience, Norton formed an all-black political association that became the basis of a career in York County politics lasting forty years. Another Virginia fugitive was Thomas Bayne, who had failed in one escape attempt in 1844 and had finally reached the North in 1855. Returning to Norfolk at the end of the Civil War, Bayne became the most important black leader at the Virginia constitutional convention of 1867, advocating, among other things, an overhaul of the state's antiquated taxation system to shift the tax burden from the poor to large landowners.

Among the most radical of all black officeholders was Aaron A. Bradley, once the slave of Francis Pickens, South Carolina's Civil War governor. Born around 1815, Bradley escaped during the 1830s to Boston, where he studied law and became an attorney. He returned to Georgia in 1865, and emerged as an articulate champion of black suffrage and land distribution. Early in 1866, after helping organize freedmen who resisted the restoration of land to their former owners, and delivering a speech containing disparaging remarks about Abraham Lincoln and Secretary of War Edwin M. Stanton, Bradley was expelled from Georgia by the Freedmen's Bureau. By the end of the year he returned, and went on to serve in the constitutional convention and state senate.

Despite the prominence of those born free or who in one way or another acquired their freedom before 1860, the majority of black officeholders had remained slaves until sometime during the Civil War. If the urban free elite in most states took the lead in political organizing immediately after the Civil War, once mobilization spread through the Black Belt in 1867, former slaves came to supplant much of the early leadership. The early lives of individual slaves are notoriously difficult to trace, but enough is known about the Reconstruction officeholders to offer insights into the experience of slavery, and to suggest the diversity of life histories encompassed within the South's "peculiar institution."

A number of ex-slave officials had occupied positions of considerable privilege, including access to education, despite laws barring such instruction. Several were sons of their owners and treated virtually as free; others, even when not related by blood, were educated by their masters or other whites. Blanche K. Bruce, the future senator from Mississippi and possibly his owner's son, was educated by the same private tutor who instructed his master's legitimate child. Alabama legislator John Dozier had been owned by a Virginia college president and acquired an extensive education, including a command of Greek. William A. Rector, a Little Rock city marshal, had been owned by Chester Ashley, U.S. senator from Arkansas, and as a youth played in "Ashley's Band," a traveling musical troupe composed of the senator's slaves. Rector was the only one to escape death when a steamboat on which the band was sailing exploded.

Depending on the goodwill of a single individual, however, the status of even the most privileged slave was always precarious. Especially when the inheritance of property (including property in slaves) was involved, the master's sense of obligation frequently followed him to the grave. John Carraway, who served in Alabama's constitutional convention and legislature, was the son of a planter and a slave mother, and was freed in his father's will. But the "white guardians" to whom their care had been entrusted had Carraway's mother sold "all for the purpose of getting possession of the property left us by my father." Carraway remained free but was forced to leave the state. Thomas M. Allen, a Charleston slave, was freed in the will of his owner-father, along with his mother and brother. But his father's relatives "stole" the family, Allen later related, sold them to Georgia, and seized the money bequeathed to them. Allen remained a slave until the end of the Civil War. During Reconstruction, he served in Georgia's legislature.

These were only a few of the Reconstruction officials who had known firsthand the horrors of slavery. Congressmen Jeremiah Haralson and John A. Hyman had been sold on the auction block. Richard Griggs, Mississippi's commissioner of immigration and agriculture, was sold eighteen times while a slave. At one point, Griggs was owned by Nathan B. Forrest, later the Confederate general responsible for the murder of black soldiers in the Fort Pillow massacre and a founder of the Ku Klux Klan. Virginia constitutional convention delegate John Brown had seen his wife and two daughters sold to Mississippi. It should not be surprising that in the black political ideology that emerged after the war, slavery was recalled not as a time of mutual rights and responsibilities, but as a terrible injustice, a stain upon the conscience of the nation.

The 1,465 officials followed eighty-three occupations, ranging from apothecary to woodfactor, and included a chef, gardener, insurance agent, and "conjurer." Taken together, the black officials present a picture that should be familiar to anyone acquainted with the political leadership that generally emerged in the nineteenth-century lower-class communities in times of political crisis— artisans, professionals, small property holders, and laborers. For some, Reconstruction prominence was an extension of leadership roles they had occupied in the slave community. Black editor T. Thomas Fortune later explained how the political role of his father, Emanuel Fortune, a Florida constitutional convention delegate and legislator, had its roots before the Civil War. "It was natural for him to take the leadership in any independent movement of the Negroes. During and before the Civil War he had commanded his time as a tanner and expert shoe and boot maker. In such life as the slaves were allowed and in church work, he took the leader's part. When the matter of the Constitutional Convention was decided upon his people in Jackson County naturally looked to him to shape up matters for them."

Like Fortune, a large number of black officeholders were artisans—former slaves whose skill and relative independence (often reflected in command over their own time and the ability to travel off the plantation) accorded them high status in the slave community—and free blacks who had followed skilled trades before the Civil War. Among artisans, carpenter, barber, blacksmith, mason, and shoemaker were the crafts most frequently represented.

Another large occupational grouping consisted of professionals. There were 237 ministers among the Reconstruction officials, mostly Methodists and Baptists, with a handful of Presbyterians, Congregationalists, and Episcopalians. "A man cannot do his whole duty as a minister except he looks out for the political interests of his people," said Charles H. Pearce, who had purchased his freedom in Maryland as a young man, served as an African Methodist Episcopal preacher in Canada before the Civil War, came to Florida as a religious missionary, and was elected to the constitutional convention and state Senate. Many of Reconstruction's most prominent black leaders not only emerged from the church, but had a political outlook grounded in a providential view of history inspired by black Christianity. The cause of the Civil War, declared James D. Lynch, a minister and religious missionary who became Mississippi's secretary of state during Reconstruction, was America's "disobedience," via slavery, to its divine mission to "elevate humanity" and spread freedom throughout the globe. Justice for the former slaves, Lynch continued, could not be long delayed, because "Divine Providence will wring from you in wrath, that which should have been given in love."

Teachers accounted for 172 officeholders, some of whom established schools for black children on their own initiative immediately after the Civil War, and 69 were lawyers, nearly all of whom gained admission to the bar after the Civil War. Seven black officeholders were musicians, five worked as physicians, and one, Thomas Bayne, practiced dentistry.

Businessmen comprised another large group of officeholders, the majority of them small shopkeepers and grocers, along with a scattering of building contractors, saloonkeepers, and hotel owners. Not surprisingly, farmer was the largest occupational category, accounting for 294 officials. Unfortunately, the census of 1870 did not distinguish between farm owners and tenants, so it is not known how many worked their own land. An additional 32 were planters, who owned a significant amount of acreage. Finally, there were 115 laborers, most of whom worked on farms, but who included a few factory operatives and unskilled employees in artisan shops and mercantile establishments.

Information about ownership of property is available for 928 black officials. Of these, a bit under a quarter were propertyless, and just under forty percent owned real estate and personal property amounting to under $1,000. Another 40 percent held property valued at over $1,000, a considerable sum at a time when the average nonfarm employee earned under $500 per year, and Southern farm wages ranged between $10 and $15 per month.[6]

The black political leadership included a few men of truly substantial wealth. Antoine Dubuclet owned over $200,000 worth of property on the eve of the Civil War. Florida congressman Josiah T. Walls, a former slave, prospered as a planter during Reconstruction. And Mississippi senator Blanche K. Bruce acquired a fortune in real estate and "the manners of a Chesterfield." When he died in 1898, Bruce was worth over $100,000. Ferdinand Havis, a former slave who served on the Pine Bluff, Arkansas, board of aldermen and in the legislature, owned a saloon, whiskey business, and two thousand acres of farm land. Toward the end of the century, Havis described himself in the city directory simply as a "capitalist."

Most black property holders, however, were men of relatively modest incomes and often precarious economic standing. Among Reconstruction officeholders, at least twenty-four black entrepreneurs, mostly grocers and small merchants, are known to have gone out of business during the depression of the 1870s. Even Antoine

Dubuclet suffered financial reverses; when he died in 1887, his estate was valued at only $1,300. Black professionals often found it difficult to make ends meet, since whites shunned them and few blacks were able to pay their fees. Unlike white counterparts, moreover, black officials who operated businesses found themselves subjected to ostracism by their political opponents, often with devastating effect. Georgia congressman Jefferson Long, a tailor, had commanded "much of the fine custom" of Macon before embarking on his political career, but "his stand in politics ruined his business with the whites who had been his patrons chiefly."

In an era when the large majority of black Southerners were agricultural laborers who owned little or no property, Reconstruction's black officeholders obviously occupied a position of some privilege within the black community. Nonetheless, measured in terms of occupation and income, Reconstruction brought about a dramatic downward shift in the economic status of Southern officeholders. Before the Civil War, the majority of state and county officials in the Southern states were slave owners, as were most of those who held important local offices, and planters, merchants, and lawyers dominated the region's public life.[7] Reconstruction profoundly altered the social origins of public officials, white and black. Artisans and laborers rarely held office in the South before the Civil War, and did so infrequently in the nineteenth-century North. Certainly, it is difficult to think of another time in American history when over one hundred unskilled laborers held public office.[8]

Ridiculed by their opponents as incompetent and corrupt, most black officials in fact proved fully capable of understanding public issues and pursuing the interests of their constituents and party. To be sure, slavery, once described by its apologists as a "school" that introduced "uncivilized" Africans into Western culture, was hardly intended as a training ground for political leaders. Looking back on the post-emancipation years, James K. Green, who served in Alabama's constitutional convention and legislature, remarked, "I believe that the colored people have done well, considering all their circumstances and surroundings, as emancipation made them. I for one was entirely ignorant; I knew nothing more than to obey my master; and there were thousands of us in the same attitude, . . . but the tocsin of freedom sounded and knocked at the door and we walked out like free men and met the exigencies as they grew up, and shouldered the responsibilities." As Green suggested, there was something remarkable about how men who until recently had been excluded from the main currents of American life "shouldered the responsibilities" of Reconstruction lawmaking. It would be wrong, however, to assume that the black officials were unqualified to hold positions of public trust. The image of the black official as an illiterate former field hand with no knowledge of the larger world has been severely challenged by the scholarship of the past generation. It must now be irrevocably laid to rest.

In a region where before the Civil War it was illegal to teach slaves to read and write, and where educational opportunities for free blacks were in many areas extremely limited, 83 percent of the black officials were able to read and write. Some slaves, as has been related, were educated by their owners or sympathetic whites. Others were taught to read and write by a literate slave, often a relative, or, like George W. Albright, a Mississippi field hand who went on to serve in the state Senate, became literate "by trickery." Albright listened surreptitiously as his owner's children did their school lessons in the kitchen, where his mother worked. A number of literate officials learned to read and write in the Union army, and others studied during and after the Civil War in schools established by the Freedmen's Bureau or Northern aid societies. Albright attended a Reconstruction school for blacks run by a Northerner, married a white instructor from the North, and became a teacher. However acquired, the ability to read and write marked many black officials as community leaders. Former slave Thomas M. Allen explained how he became a political organizer in rural Jasper County, Georgia, and was chosen to sit in the legislature. "In all those counties of course the colored people are generally very ignorant; . . . but some know more about things than the others. In my county the colored people came to me for instructions, and I gave them the best instructions I could. I took the *New York Tribune* and other papers, and in that way I found out a great deal, and I thought they had been freed by the Yankees and Union men, and I thought they ought to vote with them; go with that party always."

No fewer than sixty-four black officeholders attended college or professional school either before or during their term of public service. About half studied in the South at the black colleges established immediately after the Civil War, including Howard, Lincoln, Shaw, and Straight Universities and Hampton Institute, or at the University of South Carolina when it admitted black pupils between 1873 and 1877. The remainder received their higher education in the North, fourteen at Oberlin College, or abroad. Francis L. Cardozo received a degree from the University of Glasgow, and Louisiana legislator Eugène-Victor Macarty was a musician who graduated from the Imperial Conservatory in Paris. Among other officeholders who had at least some higher education were Benjamin A. Boseman, a member of South Carolina's legislature, who had graduated from the Medical School of Maine, and John W. Menard, who attended Iberia College in Ohio before the Civil War and went on to hold several posts in Florida Reconstruction.

Thirty-one officials, either natives of the North or men who had migrated or escaped from the slave South, were involved in the movement for the abolition of slavery and equal rights for Northern blacks before the Civil War. Fugitive slaves Thomas Bayne and Aaron A. Bradley worked with the antislavery movement in Massachusetts, and the freeborn Hodges brothers—Charles, William, and Willis, whose family had been forced to flee Virginia—were active in the abolitionist crusade and the movement for black suffrage in New York State. Five officials, including brothers

Abraham and Isaac Shadd, had been active in the abolitionist movement while living in Canada, and eight, including the "father of black nationalism," Martin R. Delany, in the 1850s had advocated black emigration from the United States. At least 129 officeholders were among the two hundred thousand African American men who served in the Union Army and navy during the Civil War. Military service was a politicizing experience, a training ground for postwar black leadership. Many not only received schooling in the army, but for the first time became involved in political activism. Such men included several officers of Louisiana regiments who protested discriminatory treatment by white counterparts, and the nine Reconstruction officials who served in the famous Fifty-fourth and Fifty-fifth Massachusetts regiments, which for many months refused their salaries to protest the government's policy of paying black soldiers less than white.

It is difficult to gauge exactly how much political power these black officeholders exercised. Black officials never controlled Reconstruction. But, as Du Bois indicated when he adopted the term "Black Reconstruction" to describe the era, blacks were major actors of the Reconstruction drama, and their ascent to even limited positions of political power represented a revolution in American government and race relations.

In the early days of Radical Reconstruction, blacks often stood aside when nominations for office were decided upon, so as not to embarrass the Republican party in the North or lend credence to Democratic charges of "black supremacy." It did not take long, however, for black leaders, and voters, to become dissatisfied with the role of junior partner in the Republican coalition, especially since the first governors of Republican Reconstruction seemed to devote greater energy to attracting white support than addressing the needs of black constituents. By the early 1870s, prominent black leaders in many states were condemning white Republican leaders who, in the words of Texas state senator Matthew Gaines, set themselves up as "the Big Gods of the negroes." Gaines organized a Colored Men's Convention to press for more black officeholders. During the 1870s, blacks in five states occupied at least one of the powerful executive positions of lieutenant governor, treasurer, or superintendent of education, and blacks served as Speaker of the House in Mississippi and South Carolina. Even more remarkable was the growing presence of blacks in county and local offices scattered across the South. With control over such matters as public expenditures, poor relief, the administration of justice, and taxation policy, local officials had a real impact on the day-to-day lives of all Southerners. On the Atlanta City Council, William Finch pressed for the establishment of black schools and the hiring of black teachers, and lobbied effectively for street improvements in black and poor white neighborhoods. Other officials tried to ensure that blacks were chosen to serve on juries and were employed, at the same wages as whites, on public projects.

Only a handful of black officials, including former slave Aaron A. Bradley, were actively involved in efforts to assist freedmen in acquiring land, or advocated confiscation of the land of ex-Confederates. Many black officials fully embraced the prevailing free labor ethos, which saw individual initiative in the "race of life," not public assistance, as the route to upward mobility. Free blacks from both North and South, many of whom had achieved astonishing success given the barriers erected against them, expressed most forcefully the idea of competitive equality. "Look at the progress of our people—their wonderful civilization," declared freeborn North Carolina registrar George W. Brodie. "What have we to fear in competition with the whites, if they give us a fair race?" A considerable number of black officeholders, however, did make efforts to uplift the conditions of black laborers in other ways. William H. Grey of Arkansas purchased a plantation in order to sell it in small plots to sharecroppers, and Benjamin S. Turner introduced a bill in Congress for the sale of small tracts of land to Southern freedmen. Other local officeholders, as planters persistently complained, sided with employees in contract disputes, failed to enforce vagrancy laws, and refused to coerce freedmen into signing plantation labor contracts.

From Petersburg, Virginia, to Houston, Texas, from the Sea Islands of South Carolina to the sugar parishes of Louisiana, enclaves of genuine black power were scattered across the Reconstruction South. Traveling through the region in 1873 and 1874, reporter Edward King encountered black aldermen in Little Rock, a parish jury in Vidalia, Louisiana, dominated by black officials, and blacks controlling the city hall and police force in Beaufort, South Carolina.[9] In some areas, powerful local machines emerged headed by black officeholders, some of whom held a number of positions simultaneously. Army veteran Stephen A. Swails dominated the politics of Williamsburg County, South Carolina, serving in the legislature, as county auditor and brigadier general in the state militia, as well as editing a local newspaper. In a remarkable number of cases, politics attracted more than one member of a family. Ninety-five officeholders were relatives of another black official— generally fathers, sons, brothers, and in-laws. Four Hodges brothers and three Norton brothers held office in Virginia, as did brothers Charles, Henry, and James Hayne in South Carolina.

Even the most powerful officials, however, were not immune to the numerous indignities and inequalities to which blacks were subjected in the post–Civil War South. Despite national and state civil rights laws, a common experience of black travelers, including congressmen and state officials, was being refused service in a first-class railroad car or steamboat cabin, and being forced to ride in the "smoking car" or on deck. Edward Butler, a member of Louisiana's Senate, was beaten and stabbed by a riverboat crew member while seeking admission to the first-class cabin. In speeches supporting Charles Sumner's Civil Rights Bill in 1874, black congressmen related the "outrages and indignities" to which they had been subjected. Joseph Rainey had been thrown from a Virginia streetcar, John R. Lynch forced to occupy a railroad smoking car with gamblers and drunkards, Richard H. Cain and Robert B. Elliott excluded from a North Carolina restaurant, James T. Rapier denied service by inns at every stopping point between Montgomery and Washington. Many black officials did not accept passively being refused equal access to public facilities. Charles S. Sauvinet, the sheriff of Orleans Parish, took a saloon keeper to court after being denied service and was awarded $1,000. When Eugène-Victor Macarty was refused a seat at the New Orleans Opera House in 1869, he sued and organized a black boycott that lasted until the theater was integrated in 1875.

Given such experiences, and the broad aspiration widely shared in the black community to construct a color-blind society from the ashes of slavery, black officials devoted considerable effort to the passage of national and state civil rights legislation. "Sir," North Carolina legislator Thomas A. Sykes wrote Charles Sumner, "if I am a free citizen of this 'grand Republic,' why am I denied privileges which are given to my white brother, although he might be the basest culprit on earth?" It was the insistence of black legislators that led five Southern states to enact laws during Reconstruction requiring equal treatment by railroads and places of public accommodation.

The frequent denial of equal access to public facilities, however, was hardly the most serious danger confronting black officials during Reconstruction. It is difficult to think of any group of public officials in American history who faced the threat of violence as persistently as Reconstruction's black officeholders. No fewer than 156 officials—over 10 percent of the total—were victimized by violence, generally by the Ku Klux Klan, White League, and other paramilitary criminal organizations allied with the Democratic party. Their number included thirty-six who received death threats, forty-five who were driven from their homes, and forty-one shot at, stabbed, or otherwise assaulted. Andrew J. Flowers, a justice of the peace in Tennessee, was whipped by the Ku Klux Klan "because I had the impudence to run against a white man for office, and beat him.... They said ... they did not intend any nigger to hold office in the United States." Thirty-four black officeholders were actually murdered, most during Reconstruction, but a few after the South's "Redemption." They included eight constitutional convention delegates and twelve legislators, most prominent perhaps Benjamin Randolph, killed in 1868 while serving as chairman of the Republican state executive committee.

Southern black officeholding did not end immediately with the overthrow of Reconstruction in 1870s. Although the Redeemers in several states moved to restrict black voting, gerrymander districts to decrease black representation, and reduce the number of elective positions in predominantly black counties, blacks continued to serve in state legislatures and local positions, and a handful managed to win election to Congress. Many others occupied patronage posts distributed by Republican administrations in Washington. Joseph H. Lee, a Reconstruction legislator, served as customs collector at Jacksonville, Florida, from the 1880s until 1913. The number of black officeholders was reduced substantially after Reconstruction, but until disfranchisement had been completed around the turn of the century, enclaves of local black power existed in most of the Southern states. Norris W. Cuney was the most powerful black politician in late-nineteenth-century Texas, his machine resting on his post as collector of customs at Galveston. Robert Smalls won election to Congress in the 1880s, served as collector of customs at Beaufort until 1913, and sat in South Carolina's constitutional convention of 1895, where he spoke out eloquently against the disfranchisement of black voters.

But if black officeholding survived the end of Reconstruction, it did so in a profoundly altered context. Local officials confronted hostile state governments and national administrations at best indifferent to blacks' concerns, and black lawmakers found it impossible to exert any influence in Democratic legislatures. Most black officials now depended for their influence on the goodwill of prominent Democrats, connections with white Republicans, and the patronage largess of the federal government, rather than the backing of a politically mobilized black community.

Many officeholders left the South after the end of Reconstruction. A number, including P. B. S. Pinchback and Blanche K. Bruce, moved to Washington, where they held federal appointments and became part of the city's black elite. William T. Montgomery, who had been a county treasurer in Mississippi, moved to Dakota Territory, where he lived among Scandinavian immigrants and became the largest black farmer in the Northwest. His enterprise failed, however, and he died in poverty in 1909. Many black "carpertbaggers" returned to the North. After being ousted from the legislature and jailed by Georgia's Redeemers, Tunis G. Campbell moved to Boston, where he devoted his remaining years to church work. James P. Ball, originally from Ohio, left Louisiana for Montana and then Seattle, where he worked as a photographer, newspaper editor, and lawyer.

The majority of Reconstruction officials remained in the South, many seeking careers in the church, education, and journalism. A number prospered in business and the professions after leaving politics. Former Speaker of the House Samuel J. Lee was South Carolina's leading black lawyer until his death in 1895. Other officeholders found their economic standing severely diminished by the elimination of politics as a livelihood. Alonzo Ransier, who had been South Carolina's lieutenant governor, was employed as a night watchman at the Charleston Custom House and as a day laborer for the city, and his Reconstruction successor, Richard H. Gleaves, spent his last years as a waiter at the Jefferson Club in Washington, D.C. Former fugitive slave Thomas Bayne abandoned politics after Reconstruction and in 1888 entered Virginia's Central State Lunatic Asylum, where he died. His disease was said to have been caused by "religion and politics."

While the men who held office scattered after the end of Reconstruction, many continued, in various ways, to work for the ideals of civil rights and economic uplift that had animated the post–Civil War era. Lewis Lindsay, an advocate of land confiscation while serving in the Virginia constitutional convention in 1868, became a leader in Richmond's Knights of Labor, and Cyrus Myers, a member of the Mississippi constitutional convention, became prominent in the effort to have Congress provide pensions to former slaves, at one point bringing a petition with six thousand signatures to the nation's capital. J. Milton Turner, who served as Missouri's assistant superintendent of education, devoted his career to winning for Cherokee freedmen a share of the funds appropriated by Congress to the Cherokee nation, finally winning his prolonged court battle in 1895. A number of Reconstruction officeholders reemerged in the Populist movement. John B. Rayner, who held several local posts in Tarboro, North Carolina, during Reconstruction, became the leading black Populist of Texas, and at the end of his life collected "Wise Sayings," intending to publish them, including: "When wealth concentrates, poverty radiates," and "God does not intend for one part of his people to feel that they are superior to another part."

When the Southern states around 1890 began to enact laws mandating racial segregation, veterans of Reconstruction were involved in opposition. In Louisiana, several former Reconstruction officials helped to create the New Orleans Citizens Committee, which filed the court challenge that resulted in the Supreme Court case of *Plessy v. Ferguson*. The civil rights impulse of Reconstruction also survived in other careers. Daniel A. Straker, a customs collector in Charleston during the 1870s, moved to Detroit, where he served as an attorney in civil rights cases, won election as a municipal judge, and took part in the movement that led to the formation of the NAACP. George W. Albright, who moved with his wife, a white teacher, to Chicago, Kansas, and Colorado after the end of Reconstruction, lived into the 1930s. At the age of ninety-one, he was interviewed by the *Daily Worker* and praised the Communist Party for nominating a black man, James W. Ford, for vice president. Former Mississippi congressman John R. Lynch wrote *The Facts of Reconstruction* and a series of articles exposing the shortcomings of historical scholarship of the early twentieth century. At a 1930 Negro History Week celebration in Washington, Lynch said, "We must make paramount the enforcement of the Fifteenth Amendment."

Today, of the nation's approximately three hundred fifty thousand elected officials, 7,480 (or 2 percent) are black Americans.[10] It is safe to say, however, that nowhere do black officials as a group exercise the political power they enjoyed in at least some Southern states during Reconstruction. I hope that this essay has helped to bring to life some of the forgotten protagonists in this nation's most remarkable experiment in interracial democracy.

Notes

Acknowledgments

1. "Second Inaugural Address," Roy P. Basler, ed., Marion Dolores Pratt and Lloyd A. Dunlap, assist. eds., *The Collected Works of Abraham Lincoln*, 9 vols. (New Brunswick: Rutgers University Press, 1953–55), 8:332.

Introduction

1. Borrowing from William G. Thomas III and Edward L. Ayers, "An Overview: The Difference that Slavery Made: A Close Analysis of Two American Communities," *American Historical Review* 108 (December 2003), 1299–1307.

2. William Wells Brown, *The Negro in the American Rebellion: his heroism and his fidelity* (Boston: Lee & Shepard, 1867), 25.

3. John Hope Franklin and Loren Schweninger, *Runaway Slaves: Rebels on the Plantation* (New York: Oxford University Press, 1999).

4. I need to take a moment to acknowledge the insightful comments of David Blight and Paul Finkelman on earlier versions of my chapter in this book, as well as Rajmohan Ramanathapillai, a colleague at Gettysburg College, for helping me to rethink African American memory through the lens of remembering trauma. I would also like to thank Gabor Boritt for providing me the opportunity to be a part of this project.

5. Edward L. Ayers, Anne Sarah Rubin, and William G. Thomas III, *The Valley of the Shadow: Two Communities in the American Civil War* at valley.vcdh.virginia.edu. The Valley of the Shadow project also won the first annual eLincoln Prize in 2001, the American Historical Association's

prize for "the teaching aid that has made the most outstanding contribution to the teaching of history," and has been named as a top five history Web site by E-Blast, *Encyclopedia Britannica*'s Internet guide.

6. Eric Foner, *Freedom's Lawmakers: A Directory of Black Officeholders During Reconstruction* (New York: Oxford University Press, 1993).

ONE: American Slavery in History and Memory

A version of this essay was delivered at the National Park Service's forum at Ford's Theater in Washington, D.C., on 8 May 2000 and is published in Robert K. Sutton, ed., *Rally on the High Ground: The National Park Service Symposium on the Civil War* (n.p., 2000). I would like to thank Linda Wood Sargent and Linda Noel of the University of Maryland for their assistance.

1. See Peter Appleborne, "Can Harvard's Powerhouse Alter the Course of Black Studies?" *New York Times*, 3 November 1996, sec. 4A, (for Gates); Lynn B. Elber, "PBS Film 'Africans in America,'" Associated Press, 16 October 1998 (for TV and slavery); Michael O'Sullivan, "'Shadrach': A Museum Piece," *Washington Post*, 16 October 1998.

2. (New Press: New York, 1998).

3. On the Civil War Memorial, see Benjamin Forgey, "A Salute to Freedom's Soldiers," *Washington Post*, 18 July 1998; *Washington City Paper*, 3 September 1999.

4. On the Library of Congress exhibit, see Hugh Davies, "Black Revolt Puts End to Exhibition of Old South," *Daily Telegraph*, 21 December 1995, International sec.; Linton Weeks, "The Continuing Hurt of History," *Washington Post*, 22 December 1995; "A Library on Tiptoe" *Washington Post*, 22 December 1995; Linton Weeks, "Plantation Life Display Revived," *Washington Post*, 4 January 1996. For information on the Amistad monument, see Ken Ringle, "Sailor on History's Seas," *Washington Post*, 23 March 2000; and David M. Herszenhorn, "A Slave Ship Reborn into History," *New York Times*, 26 March 2000. On UNESCO's slave-trade project, find Douglas Farah, "Dahomey's Royal Legacy Slowly Crumbles," *Washington Post*, 16 April 2001. For information on the National Underground Railroad Freedom Center and other such museums, see Mark Fritz, "Chasing the Mystery of U.S.'s Secret Trail," *Los Angeles Times*, 5 February 2000; and Anne Michaud, "Railroad History Put On Right Track." See also Peter Slevin, "Black History Museum Has Artifacts but no Building," *Washington Post*, 9 January 2000; "Southern Almanac: A Civil War Legacy," *Atlanta Constitution*, 10 December 2000; Steven Ginsberg,

"Fredericksburg Prodded on Slavery Museum," *Washington Post*, 11 August 2001; and Stephen Kinzer, "Planned Museum Would Lead Charleston to Its Past," *New York Times on the Web*, 14 August 2001.

5. Linda Wheeler, "Civil War Tour Guides to Address Slavery," *Washington Post*, 30 April 2000; and Patty Reinert "New Battlefield," *Houston Chronicle*, 14 May 2000; Dwight T. Pitcaithley, "Barbara Kingsolver and the Challenge of Public History," *Public Historian* 21 (1999), 9–18; Sutton, ed., *Rally on the High Ground*.

6. For information on the Lincoln Prize for the best book on slavery, see the institute's Web site at gliah.uh.edu/prizes.html.

7. Eugene Foster et al., "Jefferson Fathered Slave's Last Child," *Nature* 395 (1998), 27–28; Annette Gordon-Reed, *Thomas Jefferson and Sally Hemings: An American Controversy* (Charlottesville, Va.: 1997); Jan Lewis and Peter Onuf, eds., *Sally Hemings and Thomas Jefferson: History, Memory, and Civil Culture* (Charlottesville: University of Virginia Press, 1999).

8. For information on the Clinton apology, see William Douglas, "We Were Wrong," *Newsday*, 25 March 1998; and on conservative reaction see Leonard Pitts, Jr., "Slavery Apology Fitting and Proper," *Baltimore Sun*, 9 April 1998.

9. Editorial Writers Desk, "Race Panel's Lost Chance," *Los Angeles Times*, 21 September 1998.

10. On South Carolina, see Hamil R. Harris, "NAACP Issues Call for New Activism," *Washington Post*, 20 February 2000; "Flag-Waving Controversy," *Houston Chronicle*, 24 February 2000, sec. YO; Sue Anne Pressley, "SC Lowers Disputed Flag," *Washington Post*, 2 July 2000; and "Flag War Isn't Over at Carolina Statehouse," *Washington Post*, 15 January 2001 at washingtonpost.com/wp-dyn/articles/A6311-2001Jan15.html. On Georgia, "Georgia Lawmakers OK New State Flag," Associated Press, 31 January 2001, News sec. On Mississippi, John Head, "Culture, Notes, and News," *Atlanta Constitution*, 29 October 2000, Dixie Living sec.; Paul Duggan, "Mississippi Voters to Decide on Use of Confederate Emblem," *Washington Post*, 25 March 2001; and Dahleen Glanton, "In Mississippi, Flag Vote Shows Deep Divide," *Washington Post*, 16 April 2001.

11. R. H. Melton, "Va. Scraps Tribute to Confederacy," *Washington Post*, 21 November 2001; "Slavery 'Abhorred,' Gilmore Says," *Washington Post*, 10 April 1998.

12. Officially this is called the Commission to Coordinate the Study, Commemoration, and Impact of Slavery's History in Maryland.

13. Darryl Fears, "The Capitol's Case of Slave Labor," *Washington Post*, 19 July 2000.

14. Scott La Fee, "Grave Injustice," *San Diego Union-Tribune*, 15 September 1999; and see Mel Tapley, "'Dem Dry Bones' Get Belated Respect," *New York Amsterdam News*, 12 October 1991.

15. See Brent Staples, "Wrestling with the Legacy of Slavery at Yale," *New York Times*, 14 August 2001; and see the original article by Antony Dugdale, J. J. Fueser, and J. Celso de Castro Alves, "Yale, Slavery and Abolition," (Amistad Committee, Inc., 2001) at yaleslavery.org.

16. See Jesse Leavenworth and Kevin Canfield, "To Be Sold..." *Hartford Courant*, 4 July 2000; Ross Kerber, "Aetna Regrets Being Insurer to Slaveowners," *Boston Globe*, 10 March 2000; and Peter Slevin, *Washington Post*, "In Aetna's Past: Slave Owner Policies," 9 March 2000. Regarding California's actions, see Tamar Lewin, "Calls for Slavery Restitution Getting Louder," *New York Times*, 4 June 2001.

17. See Jesse Leavenworth and Kevin Canfield, "A Courant Complicity, An Old Wrong," *Hartford Courant*, 4 July 2000.

18. David D. Kirkparick, "On Long-Lost Pages, a Female Slave's Voice," *New York Times*, 11 November 2001; *Detroit News*, 20 October 2001.

19. For various articles discussing the reparations debate, see "Why We Did (or Didn't) Publish the Ad," *Washington Post*, 1 April 2001; Sophia A. Nelson, "We Need to Put Slavery in Its Place," *Washington Post*, 10 June 2001; and Jesse Leavenworth and Kevin Canfield, "The Reparations Debate," *Hartford Courant*, 19 June 2001.

20. For articles concerning the presentation of slavery at Colonial Williamsburg, see Michael Janofsky, "Mock Auction of Slaves' Education or Outrage?" *New York Times*, 8 October 1994, sec. 1; Leef Smith, "Williamsburg Slave Auction Riles Va. NAACP," 8 October 1994; also see 11 October 1994, *Washington Post*; "Tears and Protest at Mock Slave Sale," *New York Times*, 11 October 1994; Dan Eggen, "A Taste of Slavery Has Tourists Up in Arms," *Washington Post*, 7 July 1999; and Gail Russell Chaddock, "Williamsburg's Tale of Two Histories," *Christian Science Monitor*, 2 September 1999, Ideas sec. Also see Eric Grable, Richard Handler, and Anna Lawson, "On the Uses of Relativism: Fact, Conjecture, and Black and White Histories at Colonial Williamsburg," *American Ethnologist* 19 (1992), 791–805; Curtis James, "To Live Like a Slave," *Colonial Williamsburg Journal* 16 (1993), 14–24; "Colonial Williamsburg: Planning and Public History," *Public Historian* 20 (1998); James Oliver Horton, "Presenting Slavery: The Perils of Telling America's Racial Story," *Public Historian* 21 (1999), 29–30.

21. Leonard L. Richards, *The Slave Power: The Free North and Southern Domination, 1780–1860* (Baton Rouge: Louisiana State University Press, 2000); Don E. Fehrenbacher with Ward M. McAfee, *The Slaveholding Republic: An Account of the United States Government's Relations to Slavery* (New York: Oxford University Press, 2001).

22. W. E. Burghardt Du Bois, *The Souls of Black Folk; Essays and Sketches* (Chicago: A. C. McClurg, 1903) and *The World and Africa* (New York: International Publishers, 1947), 227, 236.

23. Lee A. Daniels, ed., *The State of Black America, 2000: Blacks in the New Millennium* (n.p., 2000).

24. See Hugh Davies, "Black Revolt Puts End to Exhibition of Old South," *Daily Telegraph,* 21 December 1995, International sec.; Linton Weeks, "The Continuing Hurt of History," *Washington Post,* 22 December 1995; "A Library on Tiptoe," *Washington Post,* 22 December 1995; "Library of Congress Scraps Plantation Life, Exhibit," *Washington Post,* 25 December 1995; and Linton Weeks, "Plantation Life Display Revived," *Washington Post,* 4 January 1996. For Vlach's own account, see John Michael Vlach, "Confronting Slavery: One Example of the Perils and Promises of Difficult History," *History News* (Spring 1999). For the book, see John Michael Vlach, *Back of the Big House: The Architecture of Plantation Slavery* (Chapel Hill: University of North Carolina Press, 1993).

25. On *Beloved,* see Ann Hornaday, "Tell Your Diamonds," *Baltimore Sun,* 11 October 1998.

26. For some background on the controversy regarding Jefferson, see Leef Smith, "Jeffersons Split Over Hemings," *Washington Post,* 17 May 1999; Leef Smith, "Jefferson Paternity Called Likely," *Washington Post,* 27 January 2000; and William Branigin, "Historians' Report Attacks Hemings Link to Jefferson," *Washington Post,* 13 April 2001.

27. Ira Berlin, *Many Thousands Gone: The First Two Centuries of Slavery in North America* (Cambridge, Mass.: Harvard University Press, 1998).

28. Ibid., pt. 1.

29. Ira Berlin, "From Creole to African: Atlantic Creoles and the Origins of African-American Society in Mainland North America," *William and Mary Quarterly* 53 (1996), 272–74.

30. Berlin, *Many Thousands Gone,* pt. 2.

31. Berlin, *Many Thousands Gone,* pt. 3.

32. Berlin, *Many Thousands Gone,* epilogue.

33. For the modern discussion of memory, see Pierre Nora "Between Memory and History: *Les Lieux de Memoire,*" *Representations* 26 (1989),

7–25; and *Realms of Memory: Rethinking the French Past,* ed. Lawrence D. Kritzman, 3 vols. (New York: Columbia University Press, 1996–1999). For a discussion of the slave trade in history and memory that parallels my own, see Ralph A. Austin, "The Slave Trade as History and Memory: Confrontations of Slaving Voyage Documents and Communal Traditions" and Bernard Bailyn "Considering the Slave Trade: History and Memory," both in the *William and Mary Quarterly,* ser. 3, 58 (2001), 228–51.

34. Norman R. Yetman, "The Background of the Slave Narrative Collection," *American Quarterly* 19 (1967), 534–52; C. Vann Woodward, "History from Slave Sources: A Review Article," *American Historical Review* 79 (1985), 470–81; Paul Escott, *Slavery Remembered: A Record of Twentieth Century Slave Narratives* (Chapel Hill: University of North Carolina Press, 1979); Charles T. Davis and Henry Louis Gates, Jr., eds., *The Slave's Narratives* (New York: Oxford University Press, 1985); Ira Berlin, Marc Favreau, and Steven F. Miller, eds., *Remembering Slavery: African Americans Talk About Their Personal Experiences of Slavery and Freedom* (New York: 1998), xiii–xlix. Most, but not all, of the narratives have been reproduced in George P. Rawick, comp., *The American Slave: A Composite Autobiography,* 41 (Westport, Conn.: 1972–1979) and online at memory.loc.gov/ammem/snhtml/snhome.html.

35. For background on the slave ship, *Brooks,* see Monica L. Haynes, "Escaped Slaves' Tales Remain Inspirational," *Pittsburgh Post-Gazette,* 19 January 1998.

36. For some background on the controversy regarding Jefferson, see Leef Smith, "Jeffersons Split Over Hemings," *Washington Post,* 17 May 1999; Leef Smith, "Jefferson Paternity Called Likely," *Washington Post,* 27 January 2000; and William Branigin, "Historians' Report Attacks Hemings Link to Jefferson," *Washington Post,* 13 April 2001.

37. For information on controversies over school names, see Ann O'Hanlon, "Racial History Fuels Growing Debate Over School Names," *Washington Post,* 10 February 1998; and "Black Begins Bid to Change School's Name," *New York Times,* 14 January 1998.

TWO: *The Quest for Freedom: Runaway Slaves and the Plantation South*

The authors wish to thank Sallie Clotfelter and Marguerite Ross Howell who copyedited, proofread, and offered many valuable suggestions in the preparation of this essay.

1. Charles C. Jones, Jr., to Charles C. Jones, Sr., 1 October 1856, in *The Children of Pride: A True Story of Georgia and the Civil War*, ed. Robert Mason Myers (New Haven: Yale University Press, 1972), 240–43; Charles C. Jones, Sr., to Mary Jones, 10 December 1856, in *Children of Pride*, 270–71. Three recent books relate to the subject matter discussed in this essay. See Edward Ball's *Slaves in the Family* (New York: Farrar, Straus and Giroux, 1998), which won the National Book Award; Walter Johnson's *Soul by Soul: Life Inside the Antebellum Slave Market* (Cambridge, Mass.: Harvard University Press, 1999), which won the Bancroft Prize; and Sally E. Hadden's *Slave Patrols: Law and Violence and Virginia and the Carolinas* (Cambridge, Mass.: Harvard University Press, 2000).

2. John Merriman to Mary Weeks, 13 November 1840, Weeks (David and Family) Papers, Special Collections, Hill Memorial Library, Louisiana State University, Baton Rouge, Louisiana.

3. Records of the Superior Court, Oglethorpe County, Georgia, *John Wynne vs. Moses Wright*, 1 April 1851, *Minutes 1847–1853*, 252–55, County Courthouse, Lexington, Georgia.

4. *New Bern Carolina (N.C.) Centinel*, 8 August 1818, in Ulrich B. Phillips, ed., *A Documentary History of American Industrial Society* (Cleveland: Arthur H. Clark, 1910), 2: 92.

5. *Charleston Mercury*, 26 March 1828, 17 April 1828.

6. Legislative Petitions, *Petition of James Brown Sr., William B. Brown, et al., to the Virginia General Assembly*, 14 December 1809, Cumberland County, Virginia State Archives, Richmond, Virginia (hereafter VSA); Records of the General Assembly, *Petition of Edward Brailsford to the South Carolina House of Representatives*, 26 November 1816, no. 100, South Carolina Department of Archives and History, Columbia, South Carolina (hereafter SCDAH); *Petition of Edward Brailsford to the South Carolina Senate*, ca. 1821, ND, no. 1838, SCDAH; *Deposition, James Hartley Hext*, 12 December 1821, with ibid.; *Deposition, Seth Prior*, 21 November 1821, with ibid.; *Petition of Edward Brailsford to the South Carolina House of Representatives*, ca. 1821, ND no. 1837, with ibid; Herbert Aptheker, "Maroons Within the Present Limits of the United States," *Journal of Negro History* 24 (April 1939), 167–68; Philip Schwarz, *Twice Condemned: Slaves and the Criminal Laws of Virginia, 1705–1865* (Baton Rouge: Louisiana State University Press, 1988), 225–26. On the difficulty of capturing runaways in the Great Dismal Swamp, see *Laws of North-Carolina, Enacted by a General Assembly, begun and held at Raleigh, on the eighteenth day of November, in the year of our*

Lord one thousand eight hundred and twenty-two [1822], 28–29; Laws of the State of North Carolina, Passed by the General Assembly, at the Session of 1848–'49 (Raleigh: Thomas Lemay, 1849), 213–15.

7. Records of the General Assembly, Session Records, Petition of William L. Hill to the North Carolina General Assembly, [1823], in Petitions (misc.), November 1823–January 1824, box 4, North Carolina Department of Archives and History, Raleigh, North Carolina (hereafter NCDAH); Report of the Committee on Claims, 8 December 1823, in House Committee Reports, box 3, ibid.; Petition of John Rhem to the North Carolina General Assembly, November 1822, in House Committee Reports, November 1823–January 1824, box 3, NCDAH; Sworn Oaths, William Boyd and John T. Boyd, 13 November 1822, ibid.; Report of the Committee of Claims, ca. 1824, ibid. A few years later in the nearby counties, a group of outlying blacks intimidated members of patrols by threatening to burn their homes. Records of the General Assembly, Session Records, Petition of residents of Sampson, Bladen, New Hanover, and Duplin counties to the North Carolina General Assembly, ca. 1830, session November 1830–January 1831, Miscellaneous Petitions, NCDAH; R. H. Taylor, "Slave Conspiracies in North Carolina," North Carolina Historical Review 5 (January 1928), 24.

8. North Carolina Minerva and Raleigh Advertiser, 25 October 1816, in Freddie L. Parker, ed., Stealing a Little Freedom: Advertisements for Slave Runaways in North Carolina, 1791–1840 (New York: Garland Publishing, Inc., 1994), 120.

9. Charleston Mercury, 18, 21, 25 November 1857; 9, 16, 19 December 1857.

10. See John Hope Franklin and Loren Schweninger, Runaway Slaves: Rebels on the Plantation (New York: Oxford University Press, 1999), chap. 9 and app. 7.

11. Deposition of James I. Dozier, 21 November 1831, with Legislative Petitions, Petition of Austin Grisham to the General Assembly, ca. 1831, no. 18–1831, reel no. 18, Tennessee State Library and Archives, Nashville, Tennessee; Charleston Mercury, 11 December 1832.

12. Richard J. M. Blackett, Beating Against the Barriers: Biographical Essays in Nineteenth-Century Afro-American History (Baton Rouge: Louisiana State University Press, 1986), 87–90; Larry Gara, The Liberty Line: The Legend of the Underground Railroad (Lexington: University of Kentucky Press, 1961), 49–50; Jenny Bourne Wahl, "The Bondsman's Burden: An Economic Analysis of the Jurisprudence of Slaves and Common Carriers," Journal of Economic History 53 (September 1993), 511–15.

13. Donald R. Wright, *African Americans in the Early Republic, 1789–1831* (Arlington Heights, Ill.: Harlan Davidson, Inc., 1993), 38–39; Michael Tadman, *Speculators and Slaves: Masters and Slaves in the Old South* (Madison: University of Wisconsin Press, 1989), chap. 1; Donald M. Sweig, "Reassessing the Human Dimension of the Interstate Slave Trade," *Prologue* 12 (Spring 1980), 5–21; Frederic Bancroft, *Slave Trading in the Old South* (Baltimore: J. H. Furst Co., 1931), chap. 15.

14. J. O. Stanfield to Betts and Gregory, 18 February 1861, Chase Family Papers, Library of Congress.

15. V. O. Witcher to Betts and Gregory, 22 February 1861, Chase Family Papers, Library of Congress. Also see T. H. Lipscomb to Browning, Moore and Company, 17 April 1860, ibid.; C. B. Ackiss to Browning, Moore and Company, 3 July 1860, ibid.; Bills of Sale, 21 March 1817, 27 March 1824, Alexander Stewart, Augusta County, Virginia, in Sterritt Family Papers, Library of Congress.

16. *Charleston Mercury*, 11 January 1831. Jim had absconded in June 1830, and the notice ran through 1 February 1831.

17. *New Orleans Bee*, 16 November 1833.

18. *New Orleans Bee*, 16, 18, 19, 20, 22 November 1833.

19. Willard B. Gatewood, Jr., ed., *Slave and Freeman: The Autobiography of George L. Knox* (Lexington: University Press of Kentucky, 1979), 48.

20. Anne Arundel County Register of Wills (Petitions and Orders) 1820–1840, 515–16, *Petition of Charles R. Stewart to the Orphans Court*, 26 July 1836, reel no. CR 63, 127–1, SC, Maryland State Archives, Annapolis, Maryland.

21. *A Digest of the Statutes of Arkansas: Embracing All Laws of a General and Permanent Character, in Force at the Close of the Session of the General Assembly of 1846* (Little Rock: Reardon and Garritt, Publishers, 1848), 944–47.

22. Legislative Petitions, *Petition of Samuel Templeman to the Virginia General Assembly*, 21 December 1809, Westmoreland County, VSA.

23. *Statement of Edward King to the Justice of the Peace*, Concordia Parish, Louisiana, 27 May 1831, Natchez Trace Slaves and Slavery Collection, Folder on Fugitive Slaves, Center for American History, University of Texas at Austin.

24. Frederick Law Olmsted, *A Journey in the Seaboard Slave States, With Remarks on Their Economy* (New York: Dix and Edwards, 1856), 160, 161.

25. Charles Stearns, *Facts in the Life of Gen. Taylor; The Cuba Blood-Hound Importer, the Extensive Slave-Holder, and the Hero of the Mexican*

War (Boston: Published by the Author, 1848), 14. The authors wish to thank Robert Paquette for bringing this pamphlet to our attention.

26. Olmsted, *A Journey in the Seaboard Slave States*, 163.

27. *Republican (Tenn.) Banner*, 27 February 1840; 28 June 1851; 1, 3, 4, 7, 8, 9, 10, 14, 16, 18, 19, 21, 22, 24, 25, 28, 29, 31 July 1851.

28. *New Orleans Bee*, 23–30 March 1833; 1–13 April 1833.

29. *New Orleans Bee*, 10 July 1833.

30. *Statistical View of the United States . . . Being a Compendium of the Seventh Census* (Washington, D.C.: Beverley Tucker, Senate Printer, 1854), 64.

31. *Population of the United States in 1860; Compiled from the Original Returns of the Eighth Census* (Washington, D.C.: Government Printing Office, 1864), xv–xvi.

32. Frederick Law Olmsted, *A Journey in the Back Country* (New York: Mason Brothers, 1860), 476.

33. Fritz Hirschfeld, *George Washington and Slavery: A Documentary Portrayal* (Columbia: University of Missouri Press, 1997), 64.

34. Olmsted, *A Journey in the Back Country*, 476.

35. Samuel Cartwright, "Diseases and Peculiarities of the Negro Race," *De Bow's Southern and Western Review* 11 (September 1851), 331–33.

36. Charles C. Jones, Sr., to Charles C. Jones, Jr., 26 March 1857, in *The Children of Pride*, 309–10.

THREE: *"Tradition Informs Us": African Americans'*
Construction of Memory in the Antebellum North

1. On African cultural influence and retentions among Northern African Americans, see William Piersen, *Black Yankees: The Development of an Afro-American Subculture in Eighteenth-Century New England* (Amherst: University of Massachusetts Press, 1988), especially 100–113; Shane White, *Somewhat More Independent: The End of Slavery in New York, 1770–1810* (Athens: University of Georgia Press, 1991), 185–206. Throughout this paper, when I refer to African Americans and black memory, I am concerned primarily with African Americans in the North and memory as it developed among black Northerners. Though it would be a false dichotomy to completely separate African Americans along a North-South line, much work still needs to be done on memory among antebellum black Southerners, slave and free. On oral tradition, see Jan Vansina, *Oral*

Tradition as History (Madison: University of Wisconsin Press, 1984); A. Hampate Ba, "The Living Tradition," *General History of Africa: Methodology and African Prehistory*, ed. J. Ki-Zerbo (Berkeley: University of California Press, 1981).

2. Gale Jackson, "The Way We Do: A Preliminary Investigation of the African Roots of African American Performance," *Black American Literature Forum* 25 (Spring 1991), 11; Vansina, *Oral Tradition as History*, 191.

3. Jonathan Crewe, "Recalling Adamastor: Literature as Cultural Memory in 'White' South Africa," in Mieke Bal, Jonathan Crewe, and Leo Spitzer eds., *Acts of Memory: Cultural Recall in the Present* (Hanover, N.H.: University Press of New England, 1999), 76.

4. David W. Blight, *Race and Reunion: The Civil War in American Memory* (Cambridge, Mass.: Belknap Press of Harvard University Press, 2001), 304.

5. Patrick Rael, *Black Identity and Black Protest in the Antebellum North* (Chapel Hill: University of North Carolina Press, 2002), 281.

6. William Cooper Nell, *Services of Colored Americans in the Wars of 1776 and 1812* (Boston: Prentiss and Sawyer, 1851); David Blight, *Beyond the Battlefield: Race, Memory, and the American Civil War* (Amherst: University of Massachusetts Press, 2002), 32.

7. On racial formation, see George Fredrickson, *The Black Image in the White Mind; the debate on Afro-American character and destiny, 1817–1914* (New York: Harper & Row, 1971); David Roediger, *The Wages of Whiteness: Race and the Making of the American Working Class* (New York: Verso, 1991); on free black involvement in racial construction, see Joane Pope Melish, *Disowning Slavery: Gradual Emancipation and "Race" in New England, 1780–1860* (Ithaca: Cornell University Press, 1998), 238–85; Pier M. Larson, "Reconsidering Trauma, Identity, and the African Diaspora: Enslavement and Historical Memory in Nineteenth-Century Highland Madagascar," *William and Mary Quarterly* 56 (April 1999), 335. Though Larson effectively challenges the universality of linking memory to identity among minorities, the racial dynamic absent in Madagascar remained in the Northern antebellum United States.

8. Marianne Hirsch, "Projected Memory: Holocaust Photographs in Personal and Public Fantasy" in *Acts of Memory*, 8–9.

9. *Colored American*, 16 September 1837.

10. *Frederick Douglass' Paper*, 13 November 1851.

11. Ira Berlin, "American Slavery in History and Memory," Fortieth Annual Robert Fortenbaugh Lecture, Gettysburg College, 2001.

12. James V. Wertsch, *Voices of Collective Remembering* (New York: Cambridge University Press, 2002), 7; Benedict Anderson, *Imagined Communities: Reflections on the Origin and Spread of Nationalism* (New York: Verso, 1991).

13. John Mack Faragher, *Daniel Boone: The Life and Legend of an American Pioneer* (New York: Holt, 1992); Michael Kammen, *The Mystic Chords of Memory: The Transformation of Tradition in American Culture* (New York: Knopf, 1991), 50; Gary Nash, *First City: Philadelphia and the Forging of Historical Memory* (Philadelphia: University of Pennsylvania Press, 2002), 7–11.

14. Bernard Rimé and Véronique Christophe, "How Individual Emotional Episodes Feed Collective Memory," in James W. Pennebaker, Dario Paez, and Bernard Rimé, eds., *Collective Memory of Political Events: Social Psychological Perspectives* (Mahwah, N.J.: Lawrence Erlbaum Associates, 1997), 131–46.

15. Maria G. Cattell and Jacob J. Climo, "Introduction: Meaning in Social History and Memory: Anthropological Perspectives," in Jacob J. Climo and Maria G. Cattell, eds., *Social Memory and History: Anthropological Perspectives* (Walnut Creek, Calif.: AltaMira Press, 2002), 22.

16. *National Era*, 22 July 1847; Dorothy Porter and Constance Porter Uzelac, eds., *William Cooper Nell: Selected Writings 1832–1874* (Baltimore: 2002), 34; William Cooper Nell, *The Colored Patriots of the American Revolution, with Sketches of several Distinguished Colored Persons: to which is added a Brief Survey of the Condition and Prospects of Colored Americans* (Boston: Robert F. Walcutt, 1855), 292.

17. Nell, *Colored Patriots*, 293–96.

18. Nell, *Colored Patriots*, 293–95; *Colored American*, 23 January 1841.

19. *Colored American*, 6, 13 February 1841.

20. *Colored American*, 27 February 1841.

21. Nell, *Services of Colored Americans*, 15, 9; Sidney Kaplan, *The Black Presence in the Era of the American Revolution* (Amherst: University of Massachusetts Press, 1989), 66. The flag was eventually given to Nell, who donated it to the Massachusetts Historical Society, where it remains. On sites of memory, see Cattell and Climo, "Meaning in Social History and Memory," 17–24; on post-Revolutionary memory, see Sarah J. Purcell, *Sealed With Blood: War, Sacrifice, and Memory in Revolutionary America* (Philadelphia: University of Pennsylvania Press, 2002); Wertsch, *Voices of Collective Remembering*, 53.

22. Nell, *Services of Colored Americans*, 5–7; *Proceedings of the Black State Conventions, 1840–1865*, Philip S. Foner and George E. Walker, eds. (Philadelphia: Temple University Press, 1980), 99.

23. *Proceedings of the Black State Conventions*, 208, 212; Gregg D. Kimball, "African, American, and Virginian: The Shaping of Black Memory in Virginia, 1790–1860," in *Where These Memories Grow: History, Memory, and Southern Identity*, W. Fitzhugh Brundage, ed. (Chapel Hill: University of North Carolina Press, 2000), 57–77.

24. *Atlantic Monthly*, 17 March 1866, 281; R. C. Smedley, *History of the Underground Railroad in Chester and the neighboring counties of Pennsylvania* (Lancaster, Penn.: Office of the Journal, 1883), 115.

25. *Frederick Douglass' Paper*, 24 June 1852.

26. W. E. B. Du Bois, *The Souls of Black Folk* (New York: Dover Publications, reprint, 1994), 2.

27. Nell, *Colored Patriots*, 380; on the efforts to end segregation in Boston, see George A. Levesque, *Black Boston: African American Life and Culture in Urban America, 1750–1860* (New York: Garland Publishing, 1994), 149–52 and 165–229; James Oliver Horton and Lois E. Horton, *Black Bostonians: Family Life and Community Struggle in the Antebellum North* (New York: Holmes and Meier, 1979), 67–76; *Jim Crow in Boston: The Origin of the Separate but Equal Doctrine*, Leonard W. Levy and Douglas L. Jones, eds., (New York: Da Capo Press, 1974). It should be noted that while individuals like William Parker, who were virtually chased out of the country, received strong support from black Northerners, black colonizationists who left the country did not generally receive the same degree of support.

28. *The Life and Writings of Frederick Douglass*, Philip Foner, ed., vol. 2 (New York: International Publishers, 1950), 254.

29. W. Jeffrey Bolster, *Black Jacks: African American Seamen in the Age of Sail* (Cambridge, Mass.: Harvard University Press, 1997), 102–03.

30. Nell, *Colored Patriots*, 27–28; Boston Police Court Dockets, located at the Massachusetts Supreme Judicial Court Archives. Crafus appears for the first time in 1825 on January 17, and ends his court activity for the year on December 20; David Gross, *Lost Time: On Remembering and Forgetting in Late Modern Culture* (Amherst: University of Massachusetts Press, 2000), 3.

31. Sylvia R. Frey, "Between Slavery and Freedom: Virginia Blacks in the American Revolution," *Journal of Southern History* 49 (August 1983), 388; on relocation of slaves, see Frey, *Water From the Rock: Black*

Resistance in a Revolutionary Age (Princeton: Princeton University Press, 1991), 174–205. Many eventually left Nova Scotia for western Africa.

32. Michael Kammen notes that "many aspects of the Loyalist experience during the War for Independence were conveniently forgotten." See Kammen, *Mystic Chords of Memory*, 50.

33. Sidney Kaplan, "The 'Domestic Insurrections' of the Declaration of Independence," *Journal of Negro History* 61 (July 1976), 249–50.

34. William D. Piersen, *From Africa to America: African American History from the Colonial Era to the Early Republic, 1526–1790* (New York: Twayne Publishers, 1996), 133; Ira Berlin, *Many Thousands Gone: The First Two Centuries of Slavery in North America* (Cambridge, Mass.: Belknap Press, 1998), 230; Benjamin Quarles, *The Negro in the American Revolution* (Chapel Hill: University of North Carolina Press, 1961); Rael, *Black Identity and Black Protest*, 263.

35. Frey, *Water from the Rock*, 174; Frey, "Between Slavery and Freedom," 376.

36. Nell, *Colored Patriots*, 236–38, 252.

37. Benjamin Quarles, *Black Mosaic: Essays in Afro-American Historiography* (Amherst: University of Massachusetts Press, 1988), 56; *Frederick Douglass' Paper*, 1 October 1852; Frey, *Water from the Rock*.

38. Quarles, *Black Mosaic*, 92.

39. "Fighting the Rebels with One Hand: An Address Delivered in Philadelphia, Pennsylvania, on 14 January 1862," in *The Frederick Douglass Papers: Series One Speeches, Debates, Interviews*, John Blassingame, ed., vol. 3 (New Haven: Yale University Press, 1985) 482, 484; "The Proclamation and a Negro Army: An Address Delivered in New York, New York, on 6 February 1863," in *The Frederick Douglass Papers*, 567; *Life and Writings of Frederick Douglass*, vol. 3, 96.

40. *Christian Recorder*, 27 April 1861.

41. William Wells Brown, *The Negro in the American Rebellion* (Boston: Lee & Shepard, 1867), 3–8.

42. Stanley Harrold, "Romanticizing Slave Revolt: Madison Washington, the *Creole* Mutiny, and Abolitionist Celebration of Violent Means" in *Antislavery Violence: Sectional, Racial, and Cultural Conflict in Antebellum America*, John R. McKivigan and Stanley Harrold, eds., (Knoxville: University of Tennessee Press, 1999), 89–108.

43. Roy Rosenzweig and David Thelen, *The Presence of the Past: Popular Uses of History in American Life* (New York: Columbia University Press, 1998), 149–57; *National Era*, 22 July 1847; on Civil War black veterans and memory, see W. Fitzhugh Brundage, "Race, Memory,

and Masculinity: Black Veterans Recall the Civil War," in Joan E. Cashin, ed., *The War Was You and Me: Civilians in the American Civil War* (Princeton: Princeton University Press, 2002), 136–56.

FOUR: *Black and on the Border*

The authors wish to note that the original spelling, often phonetic, was maintained in all of the correspondence quoted in this essay.

1. Unless otherwise stated, most of this essay is drawn from the Valley of the Shadow Web site, winner of the eLincoln Prize for 2000. Readers may view the letters and newspapers we quote at valley.vcdh.virginia.edu.

See Russell Duncan, *Where Death and Glory Meet: Colonel Robert Gould Shaw and the 54th Massachusetts Infantry* (Athens: University of Georgia Press, 1997), 63.

2. In March, Franklin's Democratic paper noted with relief that "in this neighborhood, there has, so far been no..." *Valley Spirit*, 18 March 1863, 1, col. 7.

3. Only a week later the paper admitted that "a negro recruiting officer visited this place last week and of course..." *Valley Spirit*, 25 March 1863, 3, col. 1.

4. Only four weeks later, in late April, the *Valley Spirit* ruefully noted that "some forty or fifty black recruits..." *Valley Spirit*, 29 April 1863, 3, col. 2.

5. "In any case, 45 men living in Franklin County enlisted in the 54th and another 13 signed up in the 55th..." Edwin Redkey, "Brave Black Volunteers: A Profile of the Fifty-Fourth Massachusetts Regiment," in Martin H. Blatt, Thomas J. Brown, and Donald Yacovone, eds., *Hope and Glory: Essays on the Legacy of the Fifty-Fourth Massachusetts Regiment* (Amherst: University of Massachusetts in association with the Massachusetts Historical Society, 2001), 22.

6. "Ten of Franklin's recruits came from Chambersburg, but ten came from Mercersburg, the small community..." Redkey, "Brave Black Volunteers," in Blatt et al., eds., 27.

7. Jacob wrote first, "I take my pen in hand to inform to you that I am well and all the rest of them are well we are..." Letter from Jacob Christy to his sister, May 1863.

8. "Two of the boys was made go and get there knacksack and they had to wear them to punish them for looking..." Letter from Jacob Christy to his sister, May 1863.

9. David Demus shared some of the same opinions of Boston in early May—"it is very cold here it snow and rain..." Letter from David Demus to his wife, Mary Jane, 8 May 1863.

10. Samuel wrote to his sister the next day to let her know that "we expect to move soon to north carlina" because "the rigment..." Letter from Samuel Christy to his sister, Mary Jane, 9 May 1863.

11. "We was on the sea seven days befor we gut to Camp," Samuel Christy wrote home, "and after we weas thear..." Letter from Samuel Christy to his sister, Mary Jane, 19 June 1863.

12. The men got out "of the ship and went in to it and took every thing that was good, Samuel told Mary..." Letter from Samuel Christy to his sister, Mary Jane, 19 June 1863.

13. David Demus calculated that the "the hole amont Was a boat a milion of dollars." Letter from David Demus to his wife, Mary Jane, 18 June 1863.

14. After taking what they wanted, Samuel noted matter-of-factly, the soldiers "set the town on fier and burnt..." Luis F. Emilio, *A Brave Black Regiment: History of the Fifty-Fourth Regiment of Massachusetts Volunteer Infantry, 1863–1865*, third ed., (Salem, Mass.: N. W. Ayer and Company, 1990), 40–43; Duncan, *Hope and Glory*, 90–91.

15. Shaw admitted in a letter home that "in theory it may seem all right to some; but when it comes to being made..." Duncan, *Hope and Glory*, 90–93.

16. "Providence has abundantly blessed our movement, few casualties of any kind—and our success..." Letter from Jed Hotchkiss to his wife Sara, 24 June 1863.

17. The demolition of a railroad bridge and roundhouse "were the only acts of real destruction attempted..." Jacob Hoke, *The Great Invasion of 1863: or, General Lee in Pennsylvania* (Chambersburg, Pa.: 1887), 111.

18. One great exception to the "rules of war" marked the Confederate behavior, "the carrying away..." Hoke, *Great Invasion*, 111.

19. The Confederates, on the second day of their occupation of Chambersburg, "were hunting up the contrabands..." Diary of Rachel Cormany, 16 June 1863.

20. Jacob Hoke interceded for two of his kidnapped neighbors and down in Greencastle "a few determined men..." Hoke, *Great Invasion*, 107–08.

21. A prominent Reformed Church theologian, Benjamin S. Schneck, went directly to Confederate headquarters..." The quotations on this episode from Schneck, Cree, and Heyser appear in Ted Alexander, "A Regular

Slave Hunt: The Army of Northern Virginia and Black Civilians in the Gettysburg Campaign," *North and South* (September 2001), 82–89.

22. Alexander, "Regular Slave Hunt." The Diary of William Heyser, valley.vcdh.virginia.edu/personalpapers/collections/franklin/heyser.html. The original diary is in The Kittochtinny Historical Society Papers.

23. Amos Stouffer sadly observed that "are scouring the country in every direction about Waynesboro..." Diary of Amos Stouffer, 19 June 1863.

24. A group of local whites, led by the owner of a local inn, stopped the wagons, disarmed the soldiers..." Alexander, "Regular Slave Hunt," 86–87.

25. William Christy to Mary Jane Demus, 2 August 1863. David Demus to Mary Jane Demus, 7 October 1863.

26. David Demus to Mary Jane Demus, 22 October 22 [?]. David Demus to Mary Jane Demus, 8 November 1863. David Demus to Mary Jane Demus, 4 June 1864.

27. Jacob E. Christy to Mary Jane Demus, 24 November 1863.

28. David Demus to Mary Jane Demus, 24 December 1863. David Demus to Mary Jane Demus, 24 February 1864.

29. *Franklin Repository*, 17 February 1864, 3, col. 5.

30. *Valley Spirit*, 9 March 1864, 4, col. 3; and *Franklin Repository*, 30 March 1864, 4, col. 4.

31. Jacob E. Christy to Mary Jane Demus, 13 May 1864.

32. David Demus to Mary Jane Demus, 15 June 1864. Jacob E. Christy to Mary Jane Demus, 2 July 1864.

33. Waddell Diary, 22 July 1864.

34. Waddell Diary, 4 August 1864.

35. David Demus to Mary Jane Demus, 27 July 1864. Jacob E. Christy to Mary Jane Demus, 10 August 1864. Samuel Christy to Mary Jane Demus, 3 September 1864.

36. *Staunton Republican Vindicator*, 15 September 1864.

37. Mary Catharine Powell Cochran Diary, August 1864, Virginia Historical Society. Amanda Virginia Edmonds Diary, 10 June 1864, Special Collections, University of Virginia. See Ash, *When the Yankees Came*, 156–57 for further evidence of white Confederate views that the Federal army deluded slaves.

38. Civil War Diary of Eva Honey Allen, 14, 15 June 1864, folder 4, Gilmer Speed Adam Collection, Special Collections, Alderman Library, University of Virginia.

39. Waddell Diary, 10 October 1864. See also Allen Diary, for Eva Allen's commentary on the loyalty of her servants. On the number of

runaways in Virginia during the Civil War, see Ervin L. Jordan, Jr., *Black Confederates and Afro-Yankees in Civil War Virginia* (Charlottesville: University Press of Virginia, 1995), 72–90. Jordan, citing a Virginia governmental report, reported that as of 1863, 37,706 slaves out of a total population of 346,848 absconded successfully. The number only increased in 1864. M. G. Harman, one of the largest slave owners in Augusta County, lost about half of his slaves by early 1865; see Blair, *Virginia's Private War*, 124.

40. John M. Christey to Mary Jane Demus, 10 October 1864.

41. Amanda Virginia Edmonds Diary, 25 September 1864, Virginia Historical Society.

42. Allen Diary, 5 December 1864.

43. "The Spirit of the Boys," *Staunton Spectator*, 24 May 1864.

44. David Demus to Mary Jane Demus, 24 January 1865.

45. "Negroes," *Charleston Mercury*, 12 August 1863.

46. For a comprehensive study of this issue, including documents, see Robert F. Durden, *The Gray and the Black: The Confederate Debate on Emancipation* (Baton Rouge: Louisiana State University Press, 1972). See also Richard Beringer, Herman Hattaway et al., *Why the South Lost the Civil War* (Athens: The University of Georgia Press, 1986), 368–97; George C. Rable, *The Confederate Republic: A Revolution Against Politics* (Chapel Hill and London: University of North Carolina Press, 1994), 287–92; Emory M. Thomas, *The Confederate Nation 1861–1865* (New York: Harper & Row, 1979), 290–93, 296–97; James M. McPherson, *Battle Cry of Freedom: The Civil War Era* (New York: Oxford University Press, 1988), 831–36; Gary W. Gallagher, *The Confederate War*, (Cambridge and London: 1997) 107–08.

47. Durden, *The Gray and the Black,* 101–06.

48. Waddell Diary, 16 January 1865; *Richmond Enquirer*, 3 February 1865.

49. "Negroes in the Army," *Staunton Vindicator*, 18 November 1864; "Emancipation of Slaves by the Confederate Government," *Charleston Mercury*, 3 November 1864.

50. Waddell Diary, 16 January 1865.

51. Waddell Diary, 14, 20 February 1865.

52. *Richmond Enquirer*, 18 February 1865. On whites' misunderstanding the degree to which their slaves would remain "loyal" to them, see Leon F. Litwack, *Been in the Storm So Long: The Aftermath of Slavery* (New York: Vintage Books, 1979), 3–63.

53. Quoted in Durden, *The Gray and the Black,* 206–07.

54. "Mass Meeting," *Staunton Vindicator*, 24 February 1865; and "Public Meeting," *Staunton Vindicator*, 24 March 1865.

55. Joseph Christy to Mary Jane Demus, 27 April 1865.

56. Jacob Christy to Mary Jane Demus, 29 May 1865.

57. Jacob Christy to Mary Jane Demus, 29 May 1865.

FIVE: A Stranger in the Club: The Army of the Potomac's Black Division

1. *The War of the Rebellion: A Compilation of the Official Records of the Union and Confederate Armies*, 127 vols., index, and atlas (Washington, D.C.: GPO, 1880–1901), series 1, vol. 33, 429, 444. Hereafter OR.

2. *Christian Recorder*, 7 January 1865, 30 April 1864; Diary of Colonel Albert Rogall, 19 April 1864, Ohio Historical Society.

3. Noah Andre Trudeau, *Bloody Roads South* (Boston: Little, Brown and Co., 1989), 18–19; James H. Rickard, "Service with Colored Troops in Burnside's Corps," in *Personal Narratives of Events of the War of the Rebellion: Being Papers Read before the Rhode Island Soldiers and Sailors Historical Society* (Providence: Published by the Society, 1894–1899), 18.

4. George R. Agassiz, ed., *Meade's Headquarters, 1864–1865: Letters of Colonel Theodore Lyman* (Boston: Atlantic Monthly Press, 1922), 102.

5. Noah Andre Trudeau, *Like Men of War* (New York: Little, Brown and Co., 1998), 211.

6. Diary of Byrd C. Willis, 8 May 1864, Library of Virginia.

7. *Christian Recorder*, 18 June 1864.

8. *Philadephia Press*, 1 July 1864; *Regimental Books and Papers Forty-third USCT*, National Archives.

9. *Christian Recorder*, 3 June 1865; Diary of Warren H. Hurd, 30 June 1864, Private Collection; *Christian Recorder*, 28 January 1865.

10. *Anglo African*, 6 August 1864.

11. *Christian Recorder*, 6 August 1864.

12. *Report of the Joint Committee on the Conduct of the War*, 6 vols., index, and 2 supplemental reports (Washington, D.C.: GPO, 1861–1866), vol. 4, 14. Hereafter *Report*. OR, series 1, vol. 40, pt. 1, 58.

13. *Report*, 119–20.

14. Henry G. Thomas, "The Colored Troops at Petersburg," in Robert U. Johnson and Clarence C. Buel, eds., *Battles and Leaders of the Civil War* (New York: Century Magazine, 1889), 563–64.

15. *Report*, vol. 4, 38.

16. Freeman S. Bowley, "The Petersburg Mine," in *Papers Prepared and Read before California Commandery of the Military Order of the Loyal Legion of the United States* (Wilmington, N.C.: Broadfoot Publishing Company, 1995), 29; *Christian Recorder*, 20 August 1864.

17. *Memorial of Colonel John A. Bross, Twenty-Ninth U.S. Colored Troops* (Chicago: Tribune Book and Job Office, 1865), 33; *Christian Recorder*, 20 August 1864; Diary of Warren H. Hurd, 30 July 1864, Private Collection; Bowley, "The Petersburg Mine," 29.

18. Freeman S. Bowley, *A Boy Lieutenant* (Philadelphia: Henry Altemus Company, 1906), 93; Miles Keyes Pension File, National Archives.

19. *Christian Recorder*, 20 August 1864.

20. Diary of Warren H. Hurd, 30 July 1864, Private Collection; *Report*, vol. 4, 122.

21. *National Tribune*, 30 January 1908; Bowley, *A Boy Lieutenant*, 94; *Christian Recorder*, 20 August 1864.

22. *National Tribune*, 17 October 1907; H. Seymour Hall, "Mine Run to Petersburg," in *War Talks in Kansas: A Series of Papers Read before the Kansas Commandery of the Military Order of the Loyal Legion of the United States* (Kansas City: Press of the Franklin Hudson Publishing Company, 1906), 224.

23. *Anglo African*, 17 September 1864; Robert Porter Letter, 1 August 1864, Western Reserve Literary Society: William P. Palmer Collection; *Christian Recorder*, 20 August 1864.

24. Thomas, "The Colored Troops at Petersburg," 564.

25. Bowley, "The Petersburg Mine," 34; William Gray Pension Files, National Archives.

26. Bowley, "The Petersburg Mine," 35.

27. *Report*, vol. 4, 122; Leonard Carter Pension Files, National Archives; *Cincinnati Daily Commercial*, 17 September 1864.

28. *Anglo African*, 4 March 1865.

29. Bowley, "The Petersburg Mine," 36; *Christian Recorder*, 24 December 1864; George L. Kilmer, "The Dash into the Crater," *Century Magazine*, September 1887.

30. Quoted in William Seraile, "New York's Black Regiments During the Civil War," PhD diss., City University of New York, 1977; James I. Robertson, Jr., " 'The Boy Artillerist': Letters of Colonel William Pegram, C.S.A.," *Virginia Magazine of History and Biography* 98 (April 1990), 243.

31. Isaac Gaskin Pension File, National Archives.

32. Bowley, *A Boy Lieutenant*, 100.

33. Henry Heighton Pension File, National Archives.

34. *Christian Recorder*, 20 August 1864; Rodney Long Pension File, National Archives; Isaac Gaskin Pension File, National Archives.

35. *Anglo African*, 4 March 1865.

36. *Christian Recorder*, 20 August 1864.

37. Thomas, "The Colored Troops at Petersburg," 564.

38. *Carlisle (Pa.) Herald*, 25 November 1864.

39. Quoted in James M. McPherson, *For Cause & Comrades: Why Men Fought in the Civil War* (New York: Oxford University Press, 1997), 127; Alonzo G. Rich to "Dear Father," 31 July 1864, Petersburg National Battlefield Park, folder 8; Diary of John A. Bodamer, 30 July 1864, University of Michigan, Clements Library: Schoff Civil War Collection.

40. Quoted in Joseph G. Bilby, *Forgotten Warriors: New Jersey's African American Soldiers in the Civil War* (Hightstown, N.J.: Longstreet House, 1993), 28; Michael E. Stevens, ed., *As If It Were Glory: Robert Beecham's Civil War from the Iron Brigade to the Black Regiments* (Madison, Wis.: Madison House, 1998), 170.

41. *Christian Recorder*, 18 June 1864; *Anglo African*, 4 March 1865; *Christian Recorder*, 4 November 1865.

SIX: *"The Tocsin of Freedom": The Black Leadership of Radical Reconstruction*

1. Cal M. Logue, "Racist Reporting During Reconstruction," *Journal of Black Studies* 9 (1979), 341–47; George Campbell, *Black and White* (New York: 1879), 172–73.

2. Quoted in E. Merton Coulter, *Negro Legislators in Georgia During the Reconstruction Period* (Athens: University of Georgia Press, 1968), 179–80.

3. Claude G. Bowers, *The Tragic Era* (Cambridge, Mass.: Houghton Mifflin, 1929), 364; Coulter, *Black Legislators*, 119–20, 180.

4. For the evolution of historical scholarship on Reconstruction and its black officials, see Emma L. Thornbrough, ed., *Black Reconstructionists* (Englewood Cliffs, N.J.: Prentice Hall, 1972); Eric Foner, "Reconstruction Revisited," *Reviews in American History* 10 (1982), 82–100; Howard N. Rabinowitz, ed., *Southern Black Leaders of the Reconstruction Era* (Urbana: University of Illinois Press, 1982). Eric Foner, *Reconstruction: America's Unfinished Revolution 1863–1877* (New York: Harper Collins, 1988), is the most recent history of the era.

5. The number of blacks holding different offices, and biographical information about individuals, is drawn from my book, *Freedom's*

Lawmakers: A Directory of Black Officeholders During Reconstruction (New York: Oxford University Press, 1993).

6. U.S. Bureau of the Census, *Historical Statistics of the United States,* 2 vols. (Washington, D.C.: Government Printing Office, 1975), I, 165, 468; *Report of the Commissioner of Agriculture for the Year 1876* (Washington D.C.: Government Printing Office, 1877).

7. J. Mills Thornton III, *Politics and Power in a Slave Society: Alabama, 1800–1860* (Baton Rouge: Louisiana State University Press, 1978), 297–99; Randolph B. Campbell and Richard G. Lowe, *Wealth and Power in Antebellum Texas* (College Station: Texas A and M Press, 1977), 115–21.

8. Horace B. Davis, "The Occupations of Massachusetts Legislators, 1790–1950," *New England Quarterly* 24 (1951), 92–95; Merle Curti, *The Making of an American Community: A Case Study of Democracy in a Frontier County* (Stanford: Stanford University Press, 1959), 339–41.

9. Edward King, *The Southern States of North America* (London: Blackie and Son, 1875), 113, 281, 293, 426–28, 448, 581–82.

10. Joint Center for Political and Economic Studies, *Black Elected Officials: A National Roster, 1991* (Washington, D.C.: UNIPUB, 1992).

Contributors

EDWARD L. AYERS, President of the University of Richmond, had served as the Dean of the College and Graduate School of Arts and Sciences and Hugh P. Kelley Professor, University of Virginia. His books include *In the Presence of Mine Enemies: War in the Heart of America, 1859–1863* (2003) based on the pioneering Valley of the Shadow Project: valley/vcdh.virginia.edu. His many awards include the Lincoln Prize.

IRA BERLIN, Distinguished University Professor at the University of Maryland, is founder of the Freedman and Southern Society Project and has served as president of the Organization of American Historians. His books include *Many Thousands Gone: The First Two Centuries of Slavery in Mainland North America* (1999), and his many awards include the Bancroft, Douglass, and Lincoln Prizes.

ERIC FONER, DeWitt Clinton Professor of History at Columbia University, has served as president of both the Organization of American Historians and the American Historical Association. His books include *Free Soil, Free Labor, Free Men: The Ideology of the Republican Party Before Civil War* (1970, 1995) and *Reconstruction: America's Unfinished Revolution, 1863–1877* (1988). His many awards include the Bancroft and Parkman Prizes.

JOHN HOPE FRANKLIN, Dean of African American Historians, is the James B. Duke Distinguished Professor Emeritus at Duke University. His books include *From Slavery to Freedom: A History of African Americans,* now in its eighth edition with more than three million copies in print. One of the most revered historians at work today, he is the recipient of many honors, including the Presidential Medal of Freedom and the Lincoln Prize.

ANNE SARAH RUBIN, Assistant Professor at the University of Maryland, Baltimore County, author of *A Shattered Nation: The Rise and Fall of the Confederacy, 1861–1868* (2004), co-author of the CD-ROM, *The Valley of the Shadow: The Eve of the War* (2000) and recipient of the Lincoln Prize.

LOREN SCHWENINGER is Elizabeth Rosenthal Excellence Professor and Director of the Race and Slavery Petitions Project at the University of North Carolina at Greensboro. He is the editor of *The Southern Debate Over Slavery: Petitions to Southern Legislatures, 1778–1864* (2001) and is the winner of the Lincoln Prize.

WILLIAM G. THOMAS III serves as the John and Catherine Angle Professor of Humanities at the University of Nebraska. His work includes *Lawyering for the Railroads: Business, Law, and Power in the New South* (1999) and Valley of the Shadow Project: valley/vcdh.virginia.edu. He is an Emmy nominee for "Massive Resistance" (2000) and recipient of the Lincoln Prize.

NOAH ANDRE TRUDEAU, an independent historian, previously served as a senior producer for National Public Radio's cultural programming department. His books include *Bloody Roads South* (1989), *The Last Citadel* (1991), *Out of the Storm* (1994), *Like Men of War: Black Troops in the Civil War, 1862–1865* (1998), and *Gettysburg* (2002).

SCOTT HANCOCK is Associate Professor of History and African American Studies at Gettysburg College. His book about the African Americans' engagement with the legal system in colonial Massachusetts, *The Law Will Make You Smart*, is forthcoming in 2008.

GABOR BORITT serves as the Director of the Civil War Institute and Fluhrer Professor of Civil War Studies at Gettysburg College. His most recent book is *The Gettysburg Gospel: The Lincoln Speech that Nobody Knows* (2006).